THINKING COLLECTIVELY

Social policy, collective action and the common good

Paul Spicker

First published in Great Britain in 2019 by

Policy Press
University of Bristol
1-9 Old Park Hill
Bristol
BS2 8BB
UK
t: +44 (0)117 954 5940
pp-info@bristol.ac.uk
www.policypress.co.uk

North America office:
Policy Press
c/o The University of Chicago Press
1427 East 60th Street
Chicago, IL 60637, USA
t: +1 773 702 7700
f: +1 773-702-9756
sales@press.uchicago.edu
www.press.uchicago.edu

© Paul Spicker 2019

British Library Cataloguing in Publication Data
A catalogue record for this book is available from the British Library

Library of Congress Cataloging-in-Publication Data
A catalog record for this book has been requested

ISBN 978-1-4473-4689-0 hardcover
ISBN 978-1-4473-4691-3 ePub
ISBN 978-1-4473-4692-0 Mobi
ISBN 978-1-4473-4690-6 ePdf

Cover design by Robin Hawes
Front cover image: iStock
Printed and bound in Great Britain by CPI Group (UK) Ltd, Croydon, CR0 4YY
Policy Press uses environmentally responsible print partners

Contents

Preface

Thinking collectively is a book about the meaning, implications and value of collectivism in social policy. There are many aspects of public policy that need to be understood in collectivist terms. The most obvious examples are probably defence, foreign policy or cultural development – if they are not collective, they are incomprehensible. In social policy, however, the decisions tend to be finer and more difficult. Issues like public health, provision for unemployment and education can be dealt with in many ways. There are choices to be made between individual and collective approaches, and a balance to be struck, but the options are rarely mutually exclusive.

The distinctions between individualism and collectivism are rarely as clearly defined as we might like. Some writers try to clarify core principles with invented examples, game theory, thought experiments and 'crazy cases'.[1] There may be some value in this as an intellectual exercise, but the crazier the example, the less certain it is that the principles can be applied. All the examples in this book are drawn from life; most come from social policy. Policies typically develop through a complex range of issues and negotiations, and examples drawn from experience are unlikely ever to conform neatly and precisely to the demands of theory. That also means that the lines cannot be drawn as clearly and cleanly as they might be in a thought experiment. There is no easy correspondence between theory and practice; there are policies which take individual approaches to deal with collective problems, and collective approaches to deal with individual ones. Most examples are referred to briefly. Longer examples add depth to the argument, but they also have the potential to lead away from it. They have been presented in Boxes so as not to disrupt the flow.

The issues discussed in *Thinking collectively* are far from being new, but I have been surprised to find that they have not been addressed more explicitly, or more directly, in the literature. This book is unusual, for example, in considering collectivism as a variety of approaches, rather than a unifying doctrine. The leading academic analyses of collectivism are individualistic; some contemporary criticisms of social perspectives are based on the same kind of overwrought misapprehension that greeted Durkheim's work more than a century ago. Some of the

---

[1]   R Goodin, 1982, *Political theory and public policy*, Chicago, IL: University of Chicago Press.

approaches which have had most attention, such as attitudinal research or rational choice modelling, have only a very limited connection to the issues being considered here, and for the most part they divert us from the core principles. There are critics who offer a narrow, one-dimensional view of collectivism: it is supposed, for example, to be a specific view of society[2] or a political position.[3] That hardly touches the range of collectivist arguments. In support of collectivism, the main counterbalance to individualism has not been reasoned argument, but enthusiastic and passionate calls for collective action.[4] The position I have taken here is much more cautious and subdued. Some readers may well think that the arguments in this book are plain enough – the literature on collectivism is nothing like as heavyweight, or as convoluted, as the literature on individualism – but they may also, I hope, ask themselves why they haven't seen them before. Given the amount that has been written about collectivism, I found somewhat more scope for a fresh look than ought to have been possible.

Paul Spicker
St Andrews
October 2018

---

[2] e.g. J Agassi, 1975, Institutional individualism, *British Journal of Sociology* 26 (2) 144–55, p 145; A Bouvier, 2011, Individualism, collective agency and the 'micro-macro Relation', in I Jarvie, J Zamora-Bonnilla (eds) *The SAGE handbook of the philosophy of social sciences*, New York: Sage ch 8.

[3] e.g. A Dicey, 1917, Lectures on the Relation between Law and Public Opinion in England during the Nineteenth Century, Lecture 4, http://oll.libertyfund.org/titles/dicey-lectures-on-the-relation-between-law-and-public-opinion-lf-ed, last obtained 28 September 2018; M Oakeshott, 1993, *Morality and politics in modern Europe*, New Haven, CT: Yale University Press.

[4] e.g. Common Weal, 2017, Vision, http://allofusfirst.org/vision, last obtained 28 September 2018.

About the author

Paul Spicker is Emeritus Professor of Public Policy at Robert Gordon University, Aberdeen, and a Fellow of CROP, the International Social Science Council's Comparative Research Group on Poverty. His research includes studies of poverty, need, disadvantage and service delivery; he has worked as a consultant for a range of agencies in social welfare provision. His books include:

- *Stigma and social welfare* (Croom Helm, 1984)
- *Principles of social welfare* (Routledge, 1988)
- *Social housing and the social services* (Longmans, 1989)
- *Poverty and social security: Concepts and principles* (Routledge, 1993)
- *Planning for the needs of people with dementia* (with D S Gordon, Avebury, 1997)
- *Social protection: A bilingual glossary* (co-editor with J-P Révauger, Mission-Recherche, 1998)
- *Social policy in a changing society* (with Maurice Mullard, Routledge, 1998)
- *Policy analysis for practice* (Policy Press, 2006)
- *Poverty: An international glossary* (co-editor with Sonia Alvarez Leguizamon and David Gordon, Zed, 2007)
- *The welfare state: A general theory* (Sage, 2000)
- *Liberty, equality and fraternity* (Policy Press, 2006)
- *The idea of poverty* (Policy Press, 2007)
- *The origins of modern welfare* (Peter Lang, 2010)
- *How social security works* (Policy Press, 2011)
- *Reclaiming individualism* (Policy Press, 2013)
- *Social Policy: Theory and practice* (Policy Press, 2014)
- *Arguments for welfare* (Rowman and Littlefield, 2017)
- *What's wrong with social security benefits?* (Policy Press, 2017)

A range of his published work is available on open access at http://spicker.uk

PART I

Collectivism

Collectivism is a set of ideas, principles and approaches that begin from the recognition of the collective aspects of social life. Where individualism views actions, decisions and policies from the perspective of independent, single actors, collectivism focuses on social groups, communities and the wider society.

In *Reclaiming individualism*, I made a case for social and government action in order to protect and enhance the conditions of individuals.[1] The argument of that book was based on a distinctive analytical framework, outlining three discrete approaches to individualism: moral, methodological and substantive. Substantive individualism is based in the belief that all actions are the actions of individuals, and that every social or political action is taken by individual human beings. Methodological individualism reviews economic, social and political arguments as if they are based in the decisions of people one by one; the actions of groups are understood as a whole series of individual actions, added together. (This is the characteristic approach of economic theory.) The case for methodological individualism has been argued with some force, but whether it applies depends on circumstances; sometimes it works, sometimes it does not.

The most compelling arguments for individualism are moral. As a moral position, individualism is built around the defence of each and every person: individuals have rights, and every person matters. There is a very strong case to emphasise the role of individualism in the protection of individual dignity, rights and the value of every human being.

In the consideration of collectivism, by contrast, the strongest arguments for a collective approach are substantive, and that is where this book begins. Substantive collectivism is the idea that we live not as 'individuals', but as the members of social groups, like families,

---

[1]   P Spicker, 2013, *Reclaiming individualism*, Bristol: Policy Press.

neighbourhoods and communities, and that many of our actions are done together with others in organisations, such as schools and businesses, and social institutions. People are what they are, and who they are, because they live and have relationships with other people. Families, households, communities, organisations and nations can all be treated as social units, which have interests, concerns and priorities that might be different from those of the individuals who make them up.

Methodological collectivism looks for explanations and patterns of behaviour not in the actions of individual human beings, but in the actions of groups – including classes, ethnic groups and societies taken as a whole. This is the characteristic approach of sociology; it also has an important pragmatic purpose in the development of public policy.

Moral collectivism begins from the premise that collective social groups – families, businesses, institutions, governments and countries – are moral agents; that they have rights and responsibilities, that groups as well as individuals can take moral action, and that the morality of their actions can sensibly be assessed in those terms. Collective groups bind people to each other in networks that govern their interactions with each other, mutual responsibility and social roles.

Collectivism is not a single idea, or a unified doctrine, any more than individualism is. These are perspectives, not ideologies. They lead to different interpretations of social, moral and political issues; they suggest various approaches to problems; they emphasise alternative values. They might well underpin some systems of belief, but they are not systems of belief in their own right. It makes more sense to see them as ways of thinking. This book begins from a dualist position: it is perfectly possible to be individualist in relation to some issues and collectivist about others. But collectivism is based on the perspective of groups of people, rather than individuals, and it is only from the perspective of the group that it can be adequately understood.

1

Substantive collectivism: collectivism in practice

Social behaviour

We are social animals; we live with other people. Everyone, or nearly everyone, is born into a family and soon enmeshed in a set of relationships. The vast majority of people are born into some kind of community, where people severally come repeatedly into contact with each other, have obligations and relationships to each other, recognise each other as belonging to distinct social groups, such as families, neighbourhoods or nationalities. Little or nothing about us is unaffected by other human beings – social contact is our natural state. Life is full of situations where we know there are codes, norms, rules and expectations of behaviour. The lines may be blurred at times, but the norms that govern what one does in a supermarket are not the same as the ones that apply in a school classroom; the way that a person behaves in a music concert is not how the very same person behaves at work. Our behaviour is 'socialised'. We may put the differences down to social behaviour, but in a sense, all our behaviour is social: we do personal and private things, like sleeping, eating or dressing, in ways that we have learned to do them.

The idea of the 'social' refers, in general terms, to the substantial range of norms, expectations and influences that people are subject to as part of the condition of living with and around other people. Watkins, a committed individualist, suggests that this is all subjective:

> Whereas physical things can exist unperceived, social 'things' like laws, prices, prime ministers … are created by personal attitudes. … If social objects are formed by individual attitudes, an explanation of their formation must be an individualistic explanation.[1]

---

[1] J Watkins, 1953, Ideal types and historical explanation, in A Ryan (ed) *The philosophy of social explanation*, Oxford: Oxford University Press, 1973.

There is a case for saying that social phenomena are 'inter-subjective'[2] – that they are constructed from shared views and conventions, formed over time by groups of people. There is none for saying that they are 'created by personal attitudes', as if the money in your bank account or the laws about speeding will change if only you furrow your eyebrows and think about them differently. Social 'things' – societal facts – have an existence distinct from the mind-set of any individual.[3] Laws and prices are established by common convention and understanding, but they are not less meaningful for that – any more than other intangibles, like language, finance or history. Family relationships, banking, employment and education are not the product of individual imaginations; they are part of the fabric of everyday life.

Collectivism is sometimes conflated with 'holism', a view that everything we do is shaped by society.[4] For Agassi, 'collectivism or holism' is 'The doctrine that individual ends and decisions are created by social forces; thus they are constrained by social constraints and subject to conformity with the good of society at large'.[5] Collectivism is much broader and looser than that, but holism is an important position in its own right. It has been described as the idea that 'macrosocial phenomena have primacy over individuals in explaining behaviour and cannot be redefined in terms of individual behaviour'.[6] Social constructs may 'supervene' on individual behaviour, shaping the circumstances in which those individuals operate; individuals have to adapt or adjust to those social circumstances.[7] Durkheim explained that language, obligations, moral rules, financial reality and so forth constrain individual choices:

> these types of behaviour ... are endued with a compelling and coercive power by virtue of which, whether he wishes it or not, they impose themselves upon him. ... Even when in fact I can struggle free from these rules and successfully break them, it is never without being forced to fight against them. ... most of our ideas and tendencies are not developed

---

2   P Berger, T Luckmann, 1967, *The social construction of reality*, New York: Anchor.

3   M Mandelbaum, 1955, Societal facts, *British Journal of Sociology* 6, 305–17.

4   J Watkins, 1957, Historical explanation in the social sciences, *British Journal for the Philosophy of Science* 8 (30) 104–17.

5   J Agassi, 1975, Institutional Individualism, *British Journal of Sociology* 26 (2) 144–55, p 145.

6   R Sawyer, 2005, *Social emergence*, Cambridge: Cambridge University Press, p 48.

7   Sawyer, 2005, p 92.

by ourselves, but come to us from outside, they can only penetrate us by imposing themselves upon us.[8]

That does not mean – as some of the critics of this view would have it[9] – that no decision is individual, or that people have no agency or capacity to act for themselves. Pettit, for example, complains of Durkheim's holism that 'intentional agency is an illusion, at least in those areas where social-structural regularities rule.'[10] Durkheim does not say that: he says that countering social influences is difficult, which is not at all the same thing. There are two principles here, individual agency and social influence; there really should be no difficulty about accepting both of them at the same time. The philosopher Gilbert Ryle, writing about free will and determinism, argued that there was no inconsistency in holding that there are rules, even quite restrictive ones, at the same time as asserting that people have choices as to what to do with them – his examples include the game of chess, and the rules of English grammar.[11] Mathematics, too, has firm, rather inflexible rules (except, perhaps, in Australia[12]), but anyone who imagines that there is no scope in mathematics for creativity, originality or individuality hasn't grasped what's going on.[13] Society, whose rules are somewhat easier to bend or break, offers much greater scope for diversity.

Durkheim's work excited passionate opposition in its day:

> It is true that this word 'constraint' … is in danger of infuriating those who zealously uphold out-and-out individualism. Since they maintain that the individual is completely autonomous, it seems to them that he is diminished every time he is made aware that he is not dependent on himself alone.[14]

---

[8] E Durkheim, 1901, *The rules of sociological method*, New York: Free Press, 1982, pp 51–2.

[9] e.g. Agassi, 1975; J Watkins, 1953; P Pettit, 1993, *The common mind*, Oxford: Oxford University Press.

[10] Pettit, 1993, p 132.

[11] G Ryle, 1963, *The concept of mind*, Harmondsworth: Penguin, p 77.

[12] T Revell, 2017, Laws of mathematics don't apply here, says Australian PM, *New Scientist*, https://www.newscientist.com/article/2140747-laws-of-mathematics-dont-apply-here-says-australian-pm, last obtained 28 September 2018.

[13] G Hardy (1940) *A mathematician's apology*, Cambridge: Cambridge University Press, 1992.

[14] Durkheim, 1901, p 52.

There are still individualists who argue that all social and group action must be interpreted in terms of the behaviour of individuals. The argument was forcefully made, for example, by Hayek[15] and Watkins.[16] Popper wrote that:

> the 'behaviour' and the 'actions' of collectives, such as states or social groups, must be reduced to the behaviour and actions of human individuals ... we should never be satisfied with an explanation in terms of so-called 'collectives'.[17]

Popper's argument was more of a moral protest than an analysis of society. These writers were all working in the period shortly after a major European war, and they had strong reasons for holding people personally responsible for the outrages of that war. The circumstances of the same war, however, give the lie to the claim that everything is reducible to the level of the individual. My father and my grandparents had to escape from France, but it was France that was invaded, not my family. The countries of Europe are not just a bunch of individual human beings who happen to live in a geographical area. They are collective groups with definable legal, political and social characteristics. During my lifetime, the United Kingdom has engaged in a series of armed conflicts around the world, principally a reflection of a complex network of international agreements and alliances. A focus on individuals can do very little to explain what is happening.

Social groups

Thinking about society as a whole is not necessarily the best way to make sense of social life. A society is a collective, but it is made up of lots of smaller collectives. People live and relate to each other in groups. Groups, Brown writes,

> are an inescapable part of human existence. Like them or not, they simply are not going to go away. People grow up in groups, sometimes called families; they work in

---

[15] F Hayek, 1948, *Individualism and economic order*, Chicago, IL: University of Chicago Press.

[16] J Watkins, 1957, Historical explanation in the social sciences, *British Journal for the Philosophy of Science*, 8 (30) 104–17.

[17] K Popper, 1945, *The open society and its enemies*, vol 2, London: Routledge and Kegan Paul, pp 87, 91.

groups, as engine crews, design teams or hunting parties; they learn in groups; they play in groups, in a multitude of team games; they make decisions in groups, whether these be government committees, village councils or courtroom juries; and of course, they also fight in groups, as street gangs, revolutionary cadres and national armies. In short, human beings are group beings.[18]

Social groups have three core characteristics. First, they have an identity – they are recognisable as a group. For many groups, even if individuals in the group change, some people leave or others join, the group will still be there. Groups can be formal or informal. We come into contact with formal groups all the time – schools, hospitals, supermarket chains, telephone companies, businesses, universities and so on. In this kind of organisation, it is relatively straightforward to recognise people in terms of their role or position in the group – an employee, an official, a teacher and so on. Informal groups are more difficult to identify and interpret. Families have a clear identity; ad hoc groups of friends probably do not, and nor do people who happen to be doing similar things, like hospital patients in a waiting room, or audiences. Goffman argues that we can identify and recognise all kinds of informal collective or 'teams'.[19] We can tell the difference, he suggests, between people walking together on the street, and those who are just walking in the same direction; there are little clues, tells and elements of 'performance'.[20] These are part of everyday interaction – it is possible on the same basis to distinguish categories of individuals who are not part of a group, such as commuters and tourists. But being members of a social group implies something more than the fleeting indications that people happen to be doing something together. The main issue, Brown suggests, is that 'the participants appear to be interacting in terms of their group memberships rather than their distinctive personal characteristics'.[21] Interaction, exchange and mutual responsibility cement people into groups.

The second key thing to say about social groups is that people in the groups must have some kind of relationship to other group members. It is not enough to say that people have common characteristics, like gender or disability, or even a common identity – people often

---

[18] R Brown, 2000, *Group processes*, Oxford: Blackwell, p xv.
[19] E Goffman, 1959, *The presentation of self in everyday life*, Harmondsworth: Penguin, 1969.
[20] E Goffman, 1971, *Relations in public*, New York: Basic Books.
[21] Brown, 2000, p 9.

have many such identities. Nor is it enough to say that each member has a relationship with the group as a whole – customers, or people who donate to a charity, have that much. Identifying someone as a member of a group indicates the existence of a relationship with other members – possibly a direct personal relationship, possibly a link through a network of other relationships. The existence of a social group depends on the links between people who participate in the group. People who live, work or learn together generally have that kind of connection. Saying that someone is a son or daughter, a pupil, a resident, a colleague or a citizen conveys both information about the relationship of that person to others, and usually some expectations about what people may do within the group. We can usually tell when we, or other people, are acting on behalf of an organisation – the situation is commonplace enough to hold few surprises. The same could be said about being part of other, more informal groups – visiting a family, joining a book club, attending a church – but the position there is more ambiguous: we might talk about them as a group but relate to the group's members as individuals.

The family is a social group in these terms: families are defined by the members' relationships to each other. Family relationships take different forms in different societies: there are still societies with big, family-centred households on the Roman model, ruled by a paterfamilias, but legal structures that recognise that kind of arrangement are increasingly unusual. Nuclear families are firmly established – there is everywhere a complex structure of law around them, including arrangements for recognition of the family, obligations relating to children, rules governing divorce and succession. The relationships within families are varied and sometimes difficult to analyse; the rules governing family identification are often vague. For example, there is no obvious or consistent rule about whether or not a grandparent has any say in a family, particularly in societies where divorce has become commonplace; and it is common in many societies for children to be passed between different households or families when economic circumstances demand it.[22] The central point, for the purpose of this argument, is that we recognise the reality of family structures despite the ambiguities – a family can be engaged with, supported, asked to make decisions, and so on. People might say that someone is spending time with the family, that the family is going on holiday, that the family is having a celebration,

---

[22] H Rodman, 1971, *Lower class families*, Oxford: Oxford University Press.

and so on. These are not just figures of speech. There are good reasons for treating everyone in the family as individuals as well as family members, but families are not just a collection of individuals. The family is something real in our lives. (It has been observed that younger adults tend to deny this, at least until they start families of their own, or realise that they have been landed with the responsibility for looking after an older relative. 'We are all individualists until we wake up.'[23]) Box 1.1 discusses one of the key elements in family relationships, the duties of care that family members owe to each other, and duties relating to the previous generation.

Box 1.1: The caring relationship

People in a range of circumstances – old age, disability and illness among them – need personal care: such care may include help with personal hygiene, getting out of bed, dressing, cooking, cleaning, household management and much else besides. After the foundation of the welfare state, it was often supposed that the social services – organised personal services provided by local government or voluntary sector – were responsible for social care. A landmark study of learning disability showed that the reality is very different: families carried the bulk of the responsibility, and hours of activity and engagement on a daily basis, and the services provided by statutory authorities offered only a limited supplement to the things that family carers were doing (for example, assistance with bathing – a 'social bath' – once a week).[24] Statutory services have had to learn to plan around the network of care that is provided by families, friends and neighbours.

As increasing numbers of people have come to be served in their own homes, rather than in residential or long-stay nursing care, the relative emphasis on 'informal' care has grown. Care in practice is based more on personal relationships than on formal organisations. Often the person who helps is a spouse; it may be a son or daughter, but because care is highly gendered, it is more likely to be a daughter, or even a daughter-in-law. Within families, the responsibility is liable to fall on any adult who is at hand, but it is not confined to independent adults; much of the care given to older people is given by other older people, and in some families, young children have to act as the principal carers for chronically sick or disabled parents.

---

[23]   P G Wodehouse, 1918, *Piccadilly Jim*, London: Everyman Books, p 85.
[24]   M Bayley, 1972, *Mental handicap and community care*, London: Routledge and Kegan Paul.

The caring relationship is not one-sided. The basis of informal care is 'reciprocal', though the reciprocity can be highly generalised, and if returns are made, they are not usually made at the same time, or even to the same people, as the gift. People look after older people because the older people once looked after them, because the older people looked after their own elders and because they hope to be looked after by the next generation in their turn. (Pensions, too often dismissed by right-wing individualists as a confidence trick, are based on the same principle.) But there is direct reciprocity, too: studies of the caring relationship have emphasised what older people give to families, for example, through finance, childcare and emotional support.[25]

At first sight, the core of informal care is interpersonal; it has little to do with collectivism. It may be one-sided (though it should not be assumed to be). Nevertheless, informal care in families meets the criteria for being understood collectively: identity, relationships within the group and a capacity for collective action. Its collective nature is reinforced when dealing with other collective organisations, such as health care, personal services and commercial providers.

The third property of groups is a collective capacity for action. The form of group action that is most easy to recognise is the action taken by organisations. Collective organisations are pervasive. If, in the course of the last few days, you have switched on any electrical equipment, drunk water from a tap or a bottle, taken medicine, spoken on a telephone, studied for a course of education, heard the news or used the services of a bank, you have most probably experienced contact with a collective organisation, because it is only through collective organisations that most of these things are possible. Some organisations are institutions, like schools and universities; they are part of the social framework. Some are businesses. There are businesses which are owned and run by one person, but while they are more numerous, they are not as prevalent as businesses of another kind: businesses that are corporate. Examples are banks, electricity and gas suppliers, all the main supermarkets and clothing chains, and key internet suppliers such as Microsoft, Apple, Amazon or Google. If your mailbox is anything like mine, a goodly proportion of any mail you will have received in the last month, either electronically or on paper, will have come from organisations – a firm selling goods, a

---

[25] H Qureshi, A Walker, 1989, *The caring relationship: Elderly people and their families*, Basingstoke: Macmillan.

university, local government, the tax authority. Letters which appear to come from human beings have not necessarily been written by them, if they have been written on behalf of an organisation. We are so used to encountering and interacting with collective entities on these terms that we take what they do for granted. Collective organisation is a fact of life.

In the 'new institutional economics', organisations are treated as 'groups of individuals bound by a common purpose to achieve objectives'.[26] List and Spiekermann, who are not otherwise unsympathetic to organisational perspectives, concede a great deal to reductive individualism:

> Methodological individualists are right to remind us that the social world is ultimately the result of many individuals interacting with one another and that any theory that fails to accept this basic premise rests on mysterious metaphysical assumptions.[27]

It is not so. Organisations are not just 'the result of many individuals interacting with one another'. If we try to be reductive, to interpret the actions of organisations as the actions of the individuals who populate them – what Watkins calls a 'rock-bottom' explanation[28] – we will fail, because organisations work to their own principles, rules and processes. The National Trust, the Church of England, Barclays Bank and the Walt Disney Company all have an existence distinct from their founders or the people who populate them. In formal legal terms, they are persons: they can make decisions, buy and sell things, employ people take action. Many institutions of the type have no human owners – some businesses own themselves; others are owned by other corporations. Most of the organisations we deal with are not like 'individuals' at all. There is nothing especially 'mysterious' or 'metaphysical' about the idea that groups and organisations exist, or that they have established ways of doing things. Some of the arrangements we live with depend altogether on collective institutions and organisations, and while we can learn something about them from

---

[26] D North, 1992, Institutions and economic theory, *The American Economist* 36 (1) 3–6.

[27] C List, K Spiekermann, 2013, Methodological individualism and holism in political science: a reconciliation, *American Political Science Review* 107 (4) 629–43.

[28] J Watkins, 1957, Historical explanation in the social sciences, *British Journal for the Philosophy of Science* 8 (30) 104–17.

the conduct of individuals within them,[29] many of our interactions with organisations (such as a contract, a communication, a transaction or a financial decision) are not intelligible in terms of the interaction of individuals. In a world where routine interactions with and between organisations are increasingly moderated through standardised electronic communication, individuality does not always come into it.

If groups have a recognised identity, and are bound together by a series of relationships, they can form relationships externally with other people, and with other groups. One business can own another; businesses can make contracts with governments. A married couple can make a joint claim for benefits from a government agency. A family can move house. A local community can arrange a ceilidh. A business can buy and sell goods. A country can go to war. An industrial dispute is another instance of collective action: laws in the UK, which restrict the activities of trades unions, limit their authority collectively to call strikes, even though the individuals who have joined the unions still have the right individually to withdraw their labour. Collective action in social policy is generally action by a social group, and collective action takes place within the framework of the group's structure.

Some of the literature on social policy takes a romanticised view of collective action; it offers stirring examples of people banding together to take control or form a movement.[30] The main subject matter of this book is much more pedestrian. Social groups are part of our everyday life – the actions of businesses, communal organisations, schools, charities or government are examples. To understand their role more clearly, we need to understand the besetting ordinariness of it all.

Collective action

How can a group take action? There is no collective mind; decisions must be taken in some way by the people who make up the group. There is a class of collective action that consists of the joint action of individuals, but which falls short of action by a group. People can reasonably be said to behave collectively, Isaacs argues, when they share objectives – going for a walk, singing together, applauding, painting a house.[31] She refers to a class of 'goal-oriented' collectives – people

---

[29] S Robbins, T Judge, 2013, *Organizational behavior*, Boston, MA: Pearson.
[30] e.g. S Alinsky, 1989, *Rules for radicals*, New York: Random House; P Beresford, 2016, *All our welfare*, Bristol: Policy Press.
[31] T Isaacs, 2011, *Moral responsibility in collective contexts*, Oxford: Oxford University Press, p 25.

who share a goal and take action to do it. French refers to 'random' collectives, people who happen to find themselves in the same place at the same time – a bus queue or a mob – and other 'aggregate' collectives, people who share some feature that happens to bring them together for common action.[32] But collectives of this sort, in their nature, are temporary and ephemeral; as they develop an identity and a structure of relationships, they develop the structure and the nature of a social group.

It is easiest to recognise group action when it is formalised. Within organisations, there are usually established procedures by which decisions can be made and recognised. Every corporate organisation, French argues, has 'rules of recognition', which make it possible to distinguish which things have been decided by the corporation, and which have not. The internal structure of decision making calls for a corporate structure, procedural rules and policies.[33] Formal decisions are typically made by committees or boards; there are often elaborate structures of authority, to ensure that no one acts on behalf of the organisation without having clearly delegated authority to do so. (Governments work in the same way – more on that later.) The structures of authority can be subverted – Niskanen points to the problems of capture by a self-interested bureaucracy[34] – but it cannot be assumed either that an organisation is controlled by individuals, or even that continuing authority rests with human beings. In some cases – for example, some religious foundations and charitable trusts, and arguably in the operation of the judiciary – the key decisions rest in policies made and decisions taken by people who are now dead.

Organisations are complex, and sometimes, as with human beings, not all the decisions they come to are clear or explicit;[35] but there are rules and conventions, and it is usually possible to recognise when a group decision has been taken. The situation has to be interpreted in its context; we recognise group decisions through the 'normative import' we attach to them.[36] There are many types of corporate organisation. Some are autocratic; some are bureaucratic; some are political forums, where issues have to be negotiated and bargained over;

---

[32] P French, 1984, *Collective and corporate responsibility*, New York: Columbia University Press, pp 12–13.

[33] P French, 1984, chapters 3–4.

[34] W Niskanen, 1971, *Bureaucracy and representative government*, Chicago, IL: Aldine.

[35] See e.g. M Lipsky, 1980, *Street level bureaucracy*, London: Sage.

[36] J Gonzalez de Prado Salas, J Zamora-Bonilla, 2015, Collective actors without collective minds, *Philosophy of the Social Sciences* 45 (1) 3–25.

some are simply disorganised. (I used to work in a university where financial incompetence and mismanagement had made it possible for a determined group of scientists surreptitiously to build one of the best departments in its field in the world: 'The university did not realise that we were overspending by ten times.'[37]) Then there are organisations which bring together other organisations: consortia (where distinct organisations collaborate), confederations (where each sub-unit is self-determining), federations (where decision-making is divided between upper and lower tiers) and multilevel governance. Group action, List and Pettit suggest, is 'performative'; decisions depend on the way that organisations are made up and what they do.[38]

The role of individuals within these structures is limited and constrained. There is a literature on 'organisational behaviour' in management, dedicated to understanding the way that people behave in organisational settings;[39] it draws attention to such issues as motivation, teamwork and ethical conduct. For the purposes of this book, the area of most direct interest is the collective framework, rather than interpersonal differences – the question of how collective action is even possible.

Part of the answer to that question relates to social norms. Most of us do not sit at work wondering minute by minute or hour by hour why we are there and what we are supposed to do. We might well be distracted by our own concerns, but we do not preoccupy ourselves exclusively with them – we could not do any work if we did. The nature of the work is set in terms of the circumstances we are working in. For a new employee, it can all be a little bewildering; after a little time, we do not even think about it. Participating in an organisation depends on the process of socialisation: we learn what to do and how to behave, and what we learn becomes our habit and practice. List and Spiekermann suggest that social constructs, such as employment, may supervene on individuals, shaping the circumstances in which those individuals operate.[40]

Socialisation, however, is only a partial explanation. The clue to much of what is happening in a firm rests in that innocent word, 'employee'. The work of employees within an organisation requires them to act as part of that organisation. Employees do not do everything a human being might do – on the contrary, we expect people to fulfil the role they are supposed to fill, and it can be disturbing when they do

[37] *New Scientist*, A premier league for university research?, 15 February 1992, p 22.
[38] C List, P Pettit, 2011, *Group agency*, Oxford: Oxford University Press.
[39] Robbins, Judge, 2013.
[40] List, Spiekermann, 2013.

things that are outside that role (such as propositioning colleagues, or demanding personal sweeteners to do their job). When people work within an organisation, their activity is defined not by their individual human characteristics, but by their roles. Whenever people work in an organisation, they occupy a role, sometimes several roles. The work of a police officer, a social worker, an IT manager or a social security clerk is based in the roles they occupy. To understand what the person is doing, we need to know about the role that person has, and within organisations that role is constructed from the perspective either of the organisation, or from some external organisation such as a professional body. In economics, there is a theoretical literature which tries to explain the 'principal-agent' problem, which includes the (apparent) conundrum of why the employees in a firm should ever do what that the firm wants them to do, rather than pursuing their own interests.[41] This imagines there is a problem where there may be none. People act, for the most part, in line with the roles they occupy and the norms associated with them.

The roles that people have in formal organisations tend to be rather more closely specified than those in informal groups: they depend in part on a defined range of tasks but also, crucially, on authorisation. A person acting in such roles represents the organisation. In the examples of group action given before – shopping, education, using services, buying commodities – any interaction with a person is with a person who occupies an organisational role. This also says something important about how groups make decisions. The members of boards, trusts, committees or charities, no less than employees, are identifiable, and act, in terms of their roles; they have the authority to act, a definable set of activities that can be undertaken in those roles, and very often a set of rules about when and how decisions can be authorised. Board members, judges, legislators or voluntary committees all have power to make decisions, but they have to do it in a prescribed way, or it has no effect. People who work in occupational or professional roles may well be exercising their own judgment, but that does not mean that they are operating as individuals. The choices, preferences, quirks and foibles of individuals are only directly relevant if they fall within the scope of those roles – managers, functionaries and officials who fail to recognise the distinction between personal and organisational decisions are legitimately open to criticism.

---

[41] *The Economist*, 2017, Coase's theory of the firm, 27 July, https://www.economist.com/news/economics-brief/21725542-if-markets-are-so-good-directing-resources-why-do-companies-exist-first-our, last obtained 28 September 2018.

Sociologists have interpreted the issue of 'roles' very broadly, typically in terms of norms and expectations of behaviour[42] – possibly a 'performance'.[43] Once it is accepted that there is such a thing as a group, that the group has an identity and a capacity to act, the group can act to make things happen, usually by directing or authorising people who occupy specific roles to do what is required. Box 1.2 focuses on 'voluntary' organisations, which develop to make it possible for people together to achieve a range of social objectives, usually without a conventional profit motive; the sector operates through an extensive and complex framework of rules, norms and expectations. There are many other types of group activity. An electricity company can send a bill to a consumer. A church can distribute charity to people in the surrounding area. A school can write to parents about the way their child is behaving. These statements are sometimes picked apart by determined individualists, but they have a clear meaning; we experience, and recognise, such actions as the actions of a collective entity.

Box 1.2: The voluntary sector

The voluntary sector is sometimes called the 'third sector', to distinguish it from the state on one hand and commercial enterprise on the other.[44] At other times, voluntary and other independent services are characterised in terms of 'civil society', as distinct from the state and the individual, or perhaps the state and the family.[45] Lyons defines the third sector as consisting of private organisations

'1. that are formed and sustained by groups of people (members) acting voluntarily and without seeking personal profit to provide benefits for themselves or others
2. that are democratically controlled and
3. where any material benefit gained by a member is proportionate to their use of an organisation.'[46]

This is not always true; much of the third sector is not unpaid, some third sector organisations are there for mutual benefit, and many third sector groups are

---

[42] R Dahrendorf, 1973, *Homo sociologicus*, London: Routledge and Kegan Paul.
[43] E Goffman, 1959.
[44] W Seibel, H Anheier (eds) 1990, *The third sector*, Berlin: de Gruyter.
[45] A Evers, J-L Laville, 2004, Defining the third sector in Europe, in *The third sector in Europe*, Cheltenham: Elgar.
[46] M Lyons, 2001, *Third sector*, Sydney: Allen and Unwin.

self-perpetuating oligarchies rather than democratically controlled bodies. It is not clear, either, that the sector has to be non-profit-making. If the defining element of the third sector is that it does not take profits, then charity trading, cooperatives and community businesses are not part of the third sector.

The difficulty of defining the sector is partly because of blurred boundaries: there are social enterprises that are set up as private companies, charities that operate in the public sector, private firms that take advantage of rules for social enterprise. But it is also a reflection of the diversity of the sector, which has been called 'a loose and baggy monster'.[47] The National Council for Voluntary Organisations (NCVO) reckons that there are more than 165,000 such organisations in the UK[48] – that is about one organisation for every 400 people. The four largest categories of organisation were social service providers, cultural and recreational organisations, religious bodies and grant-making foundations; together these account for about half the number of organisations. Others are concerned with a wide range of activities – among them, education, housing, environment, law, playgroups and so on.

When people form voluntary associations, they come together to achieve some kind of social or public end. (Some associations are not, of course, actively formed by anyone who is alive currently: they may have been in existence for decades, even centuries.) For most of the last 400 years, the rules for charities in the UK required them to fit into one of four categories: the relief of poverty, the advancement of education, the advancement of religion or benefit to the community. Those rules precluded certain types of activity from being considered as charities – political associations, membership groups like sports clubs or campaigns – but many of those restrictions were lifted by reform of the law a little over 10 years ago, and the primary test now is that there should be some public benefit. (The change of focus has sometimes proved challenging for institutions previously approved for the advancement of religion or education.)

The history of social policy in most countries does not begin with government, but with a range of voluntary, charitable and religious organisations, and regulation of how they do things goes a long way back. It is 1,200 years since the Council of Aachen, when the Church expressed concern about the lax practices of

---

[47] J Kendall, M Knapp, 1996, *The voluntary sector in the UK*, Manchester: Manchester University Press.

[48] National Council of Voluntary Organisations, 2016, UK Civil Society Almanac 2016, https://data.ncvo.org.uk/a/almanac16/size-and-scope, last obtained 28 September 2018.

independent charities, and decided it may need to intervene in order to guarantee standards.[49] Seven hundred years later, during the Reformation, similar criticisms were being levied at the Church in its turn.[50] That prompted either the formation of a new sort of religious organisation, or the intervention of civic authorities. The 19th century was a period where independent, mutualist and solidaristic organisations proliferated.[51] It was also a period during which a whole range of new states were established, Belgium, Germany and Italy among them, to be followed in the 20th century by Norway, Finland, Poland and many more. Those governments started to think that they ought to have a role, too. In historical terms, the modern state is a relatively new phenomenon. Government, in the terms we understand it now, came late to the party.

Society

The idea of a 'society' has been treated with some scepticism in economic and political theory. Some individualists have argued that the term is empty,[52] and conservatives suspect it is being used to smuggle in assumptions about the way people ought to behave.[53] When people talk about 'the individual versus society', it seems to imply that the individual has some kind of immediate personal relationship to a conglomerate of Everyone Else. 'Holism' is sometimes understood the same way.[54] That is not helpful. 'Society' has a much more complex, and more definite, meaning. To understand it, we need to understand about social networks.

People live in a complex, interrelated set of groups and networks – families, neighbourhoods, communities and political communities among them. The social networks that people participate in are based in interaction, but there is more to it than interaction alone, because

[49] J Brodman, 2009, *Charity and religion in medieval Europe*, Washington, DC: Catholic University of America Press.

[50] F Salter (ed) 1926, *Some early tracts on poor relief*, London: Methuen; T Fehler, 1999, *Poor relief and Protestantism*, Aldershot: Ashgate.

[51] P Baldwin, 1990, *The politics of social solidarity*, Cambridge: Cambridge University Press.

[52] J Bentham, 1789, *An introduction to the principles of morals and legislation*, Oxford: Blackwell, 1960.

[53] e.g. M Oakeshott, 1975, *On human conduct*, Oxford: Clarendon Press.

[54] A Bouvier, 2011, Individualism, collective agency and the 'micro-macro relation', in I Jarvie, J Zamora-Bonnilla (eds) *The SAGE handbook of the philosophy of social sciences*, New York: Sage.

interaction does not imply the persistence of relationships or the continuity of networks. The word that is most often used in Europe for this sort of persistence is 'solidarity'. That term is commonly misunderstood in Britain, where it is assumed to be about sentiment and fellow feeling. The idea of solidarity is not about feelings, but about relationships, and more specifically about obligations. In Catholic social teaching, it stands for the mutual obligations that each person has to others: it embraces the responsibility that family members have to each other, the obligations that people have in small groups and communities, and the broader obligations that people have to others.[55] Solidarity implies a relationship based on interdependence, exchange or mutual obligation. The position of an individual is not, then, set in opposition to a gigantic, anonymous aggregate thing called 'society'. Every person is part of a series of networks of relationships – relationships of family, friendship, community, identity and so on – expanding outwards gradually until the links are recognisably part of a wider society. Those networks are shaped by, and shape, the pattern of relationships that make up the society; and social behaviour, in turn, is formed within the framework of those relationships.

A society is more than a social group, but it can be understood in similar terms. It has an identity, it has relationships between its members, and in so far as it shares space with a country, territory or state, it has the capacity for collective action. It is possible to identify, in the broader picture, a range of interrelated networks that are definable at the level of a country or a nation. There are some elements that whole countries share, and which they do not necessarily share when borders are crossed: those elements include common arrangements for government, formal arrangements for finance and law, and the absence of barriers (such as travel or currency exchange) that may exist in relations with other countries. That does not mean either that there cannot be closer or more restricted relationships – a society is made up of them – or that a society defines the limits of such relationships. There may well be other networks, both formal and informal, which go across national boundaries – relationships such as family, culture and trading relations.

This describes the framework in which social relationships are set, but the idea of a society refers to more than the framework. The starting point for this chapter was a consideration of the ways in which people live with each other. If society is understood as a group, it is a group of

---

[55] N Coote, 1989, Catholic social teaching, *Social Policy and Administration* 23 (2) 150–60.

rather a special kind. A society sets the terms on which other groups are formed and relate to each other. It is not just a set of relationships; it is also the process through which those relationships are expressed. In some cases, social rules can be made explicitly and directly through a process of law and government. In other cases, people interacting in groups or in personal relationships will express the things they are doing in social terms – for example, in attempts to bring up children or to enforce moral rules. In others again, supervenience 'emerges' – it is the product of many people doing interrelated things in interrelated ways.[56] The rules of the game are social and collective.

Collectivism: some initial reflections on policy

It does not follow, because so much is done collectively, that we can only respond to people in collective terms. If we want to deal with people as they are, however, we need to recognise that they do live in families, neighbourhoods and communities, and that they do have relationships with schools, businesses, public organisations and so on. One of the basic tasks of developing a social policy is to determine the focus of policy – identifying who and what policies should be dealing with.[57] Some policies are directed to individuals; some are directed towards categories of individuals, such as older people; but many are not. The focus may well fall on families, households, groups, organisations, agencies, communities and regions. Collectivism is implicit in the kind of focus that is adopted in different studies: policies relating to organisations, corporate businesses, charities or governments must, in their very nature, accept to some degree the collective nature of the activity.

There are evidently many policies which are formed in terms of a collective reality – the structure of international relations, national defence, constitutional law. Stereotyping, prejudice and conflicts between ethnic groups and communities are often conceived in terms of group relations and can meaningfully be addressed at that level.[58] Policies can be directed at collective units – families, schools, hospitals, neighbourhoods, communities, organisations and businesses – rather than individuals or categories of people (categories such as women, poorer people or older people). Groups and organisations are central to the way things are done, socially, economically, politically and

---

[56] R Sawyer, 2005, *Social emergence*, Cambridge: Cambridge University Press.
[57] See P Spicker, 2014, *Social policy: Theory and practice*, Bristol: Policy Press, ch 4.
[58] Brown, 2000, ch 8.

practically. This is not about the distinction between public provision and private enterprise – private enterprise can be collective, too. There are systems where people could provide services individually or in groups. There are places where water is sold in bottles, and others where it is routed from reservoirs through pipes. There are individual systems of transport, and mass urban transit. There are personal tutors for children, but most schools educate children in groups. (The collective organisation of education is generally taken for granted in developed societies. There are alternative models for 'home schooling' which allow for an individuated response, but they are the exception rather than the norm.) It is reasonable to debate which options are best, but it makes little sense to assume that individualised choices are always superior. It all depends on what we want to achieve and what can be done in practice.

Collective action by groups is part of the everyday interactions of ordinary lives. It does not follow that policy must be arranged in terms of group action: policies might still be directed at individuals, or inanimate objects, or the climate, or anything else. But it would be a strange set of policies that never did or said anything relating to social groups such as families, businesses, social institutions, schools and hospitals, towns, regions and so on. On occasion, the assumptions of neoliberal politics are expressed so strongly in individualist terms that their proponents seem to forget that there are collective options. Discussions about taxation are taken be about personal taxation, although much income and wealth is corporate; policies to increase savings are assumed to be about people's individual bank accounts, rather than savings and stockholding by firms (a key issue in macroeconomics); policies for obesity are liable to be diverted into discussions of diet, despite abundant evidence that both the causes and the consequences of obesity are social. Part of the purpose of this book is to consider reasons for looking at policies in other terms.

2

Methodological collectivism: social science and social policy

Understanding behaviour collectively

Methodological individualism begins from the premise that relationships and social structures have to be understood person by person. Methodological collectivism, a much less familiar idea, is based in an attempt to understand the relationships between people in terms of groups and social structures. In Chapter 1, I mainly discussed circumstances where it was obvious that people were acting in groups, but there are other situations where the choice between an individualist and collectivist approach is not so straightforward. There are aggregate behaviours – things that people apparently decide to do as individuals, but when they are considered all together, add up to a change in social relations. 'Consumer demand' consists of the aggregated behaviour of lots of consumers, all acting according to their own lights. When lots of agricultural workers leave the countryside and come to the city, it changes society; but the root of that change is the behaviour of large numbers of people. The movement of huge numbers of immigrants from Asia and Africa to richer countries in Europe is having a similar effect. Teenagers with eating disorders, people who claim social assistance, women choosing to delay childbirth to take advantage of education and economic opportunities – none of them has the identity of a social group, but people in those categories can be categorised together, analysed and responded to as if they were.

There is not much difficulty about taking a collective perspective when we are thinking about established social groups, such as families, schools and businesses. Collectivism is on much less certain ground when it reinterprets actions that might seem to be individual through a collectivist perspective – domestic violence, fleeing from a war, surviving a natural disaster. In such situations, it is possible to review the position either from the point of view of individuals, or collectively. Sociologists do both – there is no obvious intrinsic merit in always doing things exclusively in one way. But while the microsociology of interactionism can be seen in individualist terms, some patterns and relationships are not really visible at the level of the individual. Without a very high level of aggregation, we would not have known that there are patterns in the incidence of suicide.[1] We could not have told that the distribution of health care works against the people whose risk of ill health is greatest.[2] There would be no point in discussing whether crime rates are greater in more unequal societies.[3]

Even if an issue could be identified as something that relates to individuals, it does not follow that focusing on individual relationships would help to understand it. Poverty, for example, is often described in terms that relate to individual circumstances – but that does not mean that they relate only to individual circumstances, and to nothing else. Poverty is usually described at a national level, and it is done that way for good reasons. It is possible to compare the situation of poor people globally, comparing individuals across the world. The data are far from clear, but they do look quite different from an approach which judges poverty country by country, or even one which weights countries according to their population size. The most basic justification for looking at poverty at a national level is that it is often at the national level that policies are made and governments take action. Let us suppose for a moment that we could not talk about countries, but only about individuals. It would be rather difficult to discuss common issues at national level, such as labour markets, economic growth, social exclusion, foreign aid or international debt; but there is no more reason to leave those out than there would be to leave out issues affecting individuals, such as deprivation, resources and rights. It would become difficult even to consider the implications for individuals. Milanovic examines the implications for international statistics on income inequality, which are usually compiled on a national basis; at the level of the individual, the data are not good enough to sustain the analysis.[4]

None of the examples I have just given refers to a social group – or at least, not to a 'group' in the sense that I have been using the term up to now. The people in these categories do not necessarily have a relationship to others in the same situation. They might not share the

---

[1]   E Durkheim, 1897, *Suicide*, London: Routledge and Kegan Paul, 1952.

[2]   P Townsend, N Davidson, M Whitehead, 1988, *Inequalities in health*, Harmondsworth: Penguin.

[3]   R Wilkinson, K Pickett, 2009, *The spirit level*, London: Allen Lane.

[4]   B Milanovic, 2009, Globalisation and inequality, in N Yeates, C Holden (eds) *The global social policy reader*, Bristol: Policy Press, ch 2.5.

relationships or solidarities that characterise a social group. References to 'vulnerable groups' or 'disadvantaged groups' do on occasion relate to recognisable groups – isolated geographical communities, the representatives of minorities, survivors and self-help groups. More typically, however, they refer to categories of people with common vulnerabilities or disadvantages – children at risk of abuse, people with learning disabilities, unemployed young people, ex-prisoners and so on – rather than groups. There may be good reasons to classify people in such situations together. If, for example, we treat 'older people' as a group, it is because the things that they experience can be understood in terms of social patterns and structures. Social responses such as pensions, housing or social care, are provided for older people as a category; the process of categorisation helps to shape the pattern of the response.

Collectivism is distinctively methodological, rather than substantive, when it treats people *as if* they were a social group. That approach rests on a somewhat paradoxical foundation: supposing that a category might be treated collectively on methodological grounds seems implicitly to acknowledge that the category is not really a collective one. A purely methodological group would not be able to undertake collective action – if it could, it would be an instance of substantive collectivism, not a methodological issue. One of the reasons why people want to treat categories of the population as if they were groups is the hope or expectation that people in those categories will accept the identification and start to act collectively. Politics in contemporary society stresses the role of a broad range of 'social movements', networks formed around a common cause, often characterised by the absence of a formal institutional structure. Activists have adopted collectivist perspectives in relation to a wide range of issues – anticapitalism, gender, sexuality, climate change, people living in rural areas and much else besides. Much of the literature on social movements is concerned with how they come about, what social factors lead to their formation or why people take collective action.[5] From the argument in the previous chapter, there is no obvious reason to think those processes are distinctively problematic: people form groups for all kinds of reasons. But there is a much more basic question that needs to be addressed: how can we be sure, if people avoid formal structures, that a group or movement has been formed at all? Box 2.1 considers disability as a collective concept. Disability can be represented as a class; there are certainly groups that

---

[5]   D Della Porta, M Diani, 2006, *Social movements: An introduction*, Oxford: Blackwell.

claim to speak for or represent disability as a social movement; but the lack of group identity, membership or institutional structure makes it difficult to say whether disability can, or cannot, be thought of as a movement.

The position of women offers another illustration. Feminism is not a single movement, or a unitary cause. 'Liberal feminism' might be thought of as an instance of methodological collectivism. Liberal feminism refers to women as a bloc, but it focuses on outcomes for individuals; the main approaches advocated by liberal feminists are concerned with equalising opportunities for women, overcoming barriers and correcting imbalances. At the same time, there is some support for the idea that women in this situation do think of women as a group; they identify themselves with other women, they attribute their position to social relationships, and the more true that is, the more likely they are to think in terms of collective action.[6] Other feminist arguments are framed more directly as a collectivist discourse, identifying common structures, relationships and experiences that affect all women. Marxist feminists interpret gender relationships in terms of women's relationship to the means of production.[7] Radical feminists take the view that gender relationships are structured through power and patriarchy.[8] There are direct references to gender roles[9] – the same sort of construction of social relationships, norms and expectations that is found in group membership. In these models, a collectivised view of women needs to be understood not as a methodology but as a substantive reality.

Box 2.1: Disability

Disability refers to a wide range of unconnected conditions and circumstances; blindness, chronic mental illness, respiratory disease or disfigurement might all be thought of as 'disabling', but if so, they are disabling in very different ways. The World Health Organization distinguishes three elements in disability: problems in bodily function or structure, problems relating to activities and problems

---

6   R Brown, 2000, *Group processes*, Oxford: Blackwell, pp 238–40.

7   e.g. E Wilson, 1977, *Women and the welfare state*, London: Tavistock; M Barrett, 1988, *Women's oppression today*, London: Verso; but see H Hartmann, 1995, The unhappy marriage of Marxism and feminism, in D Tallack (ed) *Critical theory: A reader*, New York: Harvester Wheatsheaf.

8   J Mitchell, 1971, *Women's estate*, Harmondsworth: Penguin; K Millett, 1977, *Sexual politics*, London: Virago.

9   L Lindsay, 2015, *Gender roles: A sociological perspective*, London: Routledge.

related to social participation.[10] The 'social model of disability' favoured by many advocacy groups emphasises the disadvantage created by society; functional limitations in abilities to see distances or to run are not thought of as 'disabilities' because society allows people to function regardless, but people who are constrained to use wheelchairs or who have difficulties reaching up or down may be severely constrained by their social environment.

In general, there is a lack of recognition of commonality among people with disabilities. It cannot be assumed that disabled people share an identity: fully three quarters of the people who might reasonably be described as 'disabled' say that they are not disabled, or that they are disabled 'sometimes'.[11] Disability does not imply a common experience. The potential for different conditions to disable a person depends in part on the social environment; some disabling conditions fluctuate; some conditions, such as chronic pain or an inability to sustain physical effort, are debilitating but not necessarily recognised as disabling; and some people do not identify themselves as disabled, because other aspects of their lives are more important to them. There are sometimes references to a 'disabled community', but it is not really a community; when the phrase is used, for example, in an advertisement for a firm 'supplying a huge range of mobility aids to the local elderly and disabled community of Birmingham', it is only a figure of speech, referring to people with disabilities within a larger community.

The lack of a common identity membership does not mean that people with disabilities cannot be treated as if they were a group – that phrase, 'as if', being the hallmark of methodological collectivism. There is a 'disability movement' which argues for greater equality and social change;[12] that movement largely consists of collective groups. There are many groups for people with disabilities, offering mutual support and representation for people with common problems. In their nature, representative groups tend to take a stronger position than the groups they represent, because the people who come together to form them are more activist and feel more strongly than those who do not participate. Such groups have often been very effective, helping to change public perceptions of the people they speak for; but, by the same token, they do not simply mirror the characteristics of their supposed constituency. There have been criticisms, for example, of organisations for blind people. They tend to be dominated by

---

[10] World Health Organization, 2000, ICIDH-2, Geneva: WHO.

[11] Office for National Statistics, 2013, https://www.gov.uk/government/uploads/system/uploads/attachment_data/file/210030/q1-2013-data.xls, tables 10 and 11; last obtained 28 September 2018.

[12] M Oliver, 1990, *The politics of disablement*, Basingstoke: Macmillan.

highly skilled people who have been blind all their lives and have had specialist education, and the organisations have not always represented the needs of most blind people, who lose their sight in later life.[13]

The effect of collective action by representative groups has been to increase awareness of the issues, to encourage changes in the way that many things in the public sphere are organised, and to develop a range of services both locally and nationally that are designed to assist people with disabilities. The effectiveness of such groups depends less on their collective credentials than it does on their capacity to influence political discussion. On one hand, some of the early forms of collective action found it difficult to make headway. The literature on the 'disability movement' in the UK claims it started in the 1960s or '70s,[14] and that gives the impression that disabled people were not speaking for themselves before then. This is not true – it ignores the activism which followed the First World War, such as the British Limbless Ex-Servicemen Association[15] or the *Cripples' Journal*, itself a remarkable exercise in voice – but it is true that their political impact was disappointingly limited. On the other hand, there is the later success of a small but influential number of activists. At its inception in the 1960s, the Disablement Income Group in the UK largely consisted of two women; one of them, Megan du Boisson, lobbied civil servants and ministers in Whitehall from her wheelchair about the lack of support for people with disabilities.

That lobby was to have a powerful effect in encouraging the treatment of disability as a unifying category. When Parliament introduced an Attendance Allowance, it was intended – despite its misleading name – to introduce a general income supplement for people with severe disabilities, recognising that the incomes of people with disabilities were consistently lower than for others. Alf Morris MP, supporting the Bill, explained:

> This provision must be seen as only part – a very minor part – of an entirely new financial deal for the severely disabled. ... This is only one stage towards improving the financial status, and therefore the dignity, of every one of our severely disabled fellow citizens.[16]

---

[13] R Scott, 1969, *The making of blind men*, New York: Russell Sage Foundation.

[14] M Oliver, 1997, The disability movement is a new social movement!, *Community Development Journal* 32 (3) 244–251.

[15] See e.g. S Koven, 1994, Remembering and dismemberment: crippled children, wounded soldiers and the Great War in Great Britain, *American Historial Review* 99 (4) 1167–1202, pp 1200–2.

[16] Hansard, 10 and 15 Jul, 1970.

Peter Townsend has argued that disabled people should be seen as a 'class', a group of people who share common characteristics, identities and economic position.[17]

The attempt to think about social relationships in collective terms is often misunderstood by reductive individualists, who claim that collectivists must be rejecting all forms of individual agency, that they are being 'metaphysical', that they are 'reifying' social issues or otherwise being irrational. The whole point of methodological collectivism is that it offers a different way of looking at the world from individualism. When Durkheim looked at the problem of suicide, he did not say that individuals had no part in the process. He was interested, instead, in the ways in which a range of disparate personal behaviours could take on collectively the character of a social phenomenon, one which could not be explained, or even identified, at the level of the individual.[18] Suicide was an example of 'emergence' – the idea that even if the action is undertaken by individuals, it takes on a different aspect when it is viewed collectively.[19]

There is not much point in trying to review everything that could be said about the analytical purpose of collectivism. That would be pretty much equivalent to a discussion of the entire field of sociology. 'Sociology', Giddens writes, 'is the study of human social life, groups and societies. ... The scope of sociology is extremely wide, ranging from the analysis of passing encounters between individuals in the street up to the investigation of global social processes.'[20] That covers everything from individual interaction through to collective action. Some sociological arguments treat social behaviour as emergent; 'elisionists' claim that individual behaviour and collective group behaviour cannot meaningfully be separated. I lean to the 'dualist' approach – accepting that actions might be individual or collective, because we do both – but it often makes sense to argue that many actions are social, to the extent that they are wholly dependent on a social context, without being either purely individual or purely collective. Treating them as collective phenomena is a methodological choice – a little like the process of analysing waves rather than particles; and that is why sociological enquiry is principally an exercise in methodological, rather than substantive, collectivism.

---

[17] P Townsend, 1979, *Poverty in the United Kingdom*, Harmondsworth: Penguin.
[18] Durkheim, 1897.
[19] R Sawyer, 2005, *Social emergence*, Cambridge: Cambridge University Press, pp 2–5.
[20] A Giddens, 1989, *Sociology*, Cambridge: Polity, pp 7–8.

Methodological collectivism in practice

The methodology of collectivism in sociology has mainly been understood as a way of understanding and analysing social relationships, but there are other reasons for dealing with people collectively. That is true even if they are not clearly formed into groups and are not able to take collective action.

Here are some examples. The first is the national introduction of school meals in British schools. When the British Empire was recruiting soldiers for the Boer War, the authorities discovered that a third of the people who were medically examined were considered unfit to serve. There were concerns expressed about 'national efficiency'. The reasons for unfitness might have been treated as the responsibility of individuals and families, in the same way as income and housing were at that time; but defence, as is often the case, is a collective issue. The problem was interpreted, not as a question of the individual choices and inadequacies of parents or children, but as a collective concern. The policy response was also collective: the introduction, in 1906, of a school meals service, to ensure that young children would be more adequately fed.[21]

The second example is vaccination. In order to reduce the prevalence of certain infectious diseases in the whole population, it is necessary to reduce the exposure of large numbers of people to the disease; that protects the situation both of individuals, and of the whole population. 'Herd immunity' is achieved when the disease does not have the scope to spread, because there are no effective hosts for it. As a rough estimate, herd immunity in relation to measles – once a killing disease – is achieved when about 92–6% of the population have been vaccinated; for mumps, which is less infective, the range is 88–92%.[22] Figures vary in different countries, because the conditions for transmission are different.

A third example is child abuse. This looks to be the most individual of problems; it happens typically because of the behaviour of specific individual parents, in very small numbers, towards their children. But it has been argued that child abuse would be dealt with more effectively if it was tackled as an institutional problem.[23] Many people in the UK still think that it is morally acceptable, and even morally desirable, to hit their children in order to instil discipline. It is difficult to see why this should be acceptable for children when it is not acceptable to do it to adults,

---

[21] J Hay, 1983, *The origins of the Liberal welfare reforms 1906–1914*, Basingstoke: Macmillan.

[22] R Anderson, R May, 1985, Vaccination and herd immunity to infectious diseases, *Nature* 318 (28) 323–9.

[23] M G Sheppard, 1982, *Perceptions of child abuse*, Norwich: University of East Anglia.

and in relation to discipline, there are good reasons to think that it has the opposite effect from its intention, but that is not why I am raising the example in a book about collectivism. Methodological collectivism raises a very different kind of argument; it implies that we should treat people who hit their children as if they were a group. Because some families still use physical punishment routinely, some use it to excess. Sheppard argues that, by changing people's socialisation about domestic violence – most obviously, by making physical punishment of children unacceptable or criminal – it should be possible to 'shift the curve', altering the way that parents behave towards children, and consequently marking out cases where parents beat children to excess as more clearly deviant. That process has been happening in Britain over the last 40 or 50 years. Corporal punishment is no longer used in schools (as a schoolboy, I was hit with a tawse, a postal tube or a chair leg), and it is less acceptable than it was for parents to hit children with an implement, but we still have a way to go.

These are three very different examples; the point of bringing them together is as much to point to the contrast between them as to illustrate the importance of a collective approach. The first example, the introduction of school meals, was based on a politicised, highly ideological view of society: national efficiency was a doctrine defining the social group in terms of the British nation and indeed of the Empire. The second example, vaccination for herd immunity, might be modelled in terms of individual interactions, but that is not the central issue: the most basic precept of public health medicine is that the health of some affects the health of others. Public health consequently depends on the treatment of populations as a group. The third example shares a similarly broad definition of the nature of the group, but the approach is different again; it is directed to the process of socialisation, in the belief that social processes require social responses.

All the examples are to some extent pragmatic. Given a choice between dealing with the issues one by one or as a whole, they take the issues as a whole, and the solution that is opted for is applied to a population of interest. In each case, there are contrasting approaches that might have been taken instead. The problems of nutrition have often been dealt with through individualised policies such as information and dietary advice: that is the current approach to obesity. The problems of infection can be dealt with in an individualised way: that is why people in poor countries are routinely being issued with mosquito nets, to deal with malaria. And child abuse has long been dealt with by the questionably effective commitment to personalised social work intervention with families.

The other common feature of the three examples is that they are 'universalist', in the sense that is most commonly used in social policy: they are based on broad categories of people, and do not try to identify exactly which people within the relevant categories ought to be targeted or selected. They are not individuated or 'personalised'. There might be selective alternatives in some cases – means-tested support for family incomes, individualised health education and social work intervention. Universality is often condemned as an 'inefficient' approach – necessarily it includes provision for some who do not need it, and that implies a degree of 'deadweight', where programme interventions use resources that might have been used elsewhere. Universality is widely practised nevertheless, because the alternative is usually worse. The process of selectivity – identifying who is part of the target group, and excluding those who are not – adds to the burden and cost of administration; creates problems, inefficiency and unfairness at the boundaries; and reduces the effectiveness of policy, because there are always errors of inclusion and exclusion. But selectivity implies that responses will be tailored to personal circumstances, and the point of methodological collectivism is that it works with categories and groups, not individuals. Collective policies are not all universalist, but if we are going to start dealing with people in groups, it is possible (and may be advantageous) to address the circumstances of the group rather than trying to discriminate between group members.

The examples can reasonably be considered to be methodological rather than substantive in nature. They are not dealing with the substantive implications of collective organisations or institutions. The issues might be treated collectively or individually; in the development of policy, choices have been made to apply a collective rather than individualised strategy. There are many policies which may reasonably be taken to fall into the sphere either of individual action, or of collective action – issues such as public health, economic organisation, policy for the arts or social protection – because these are fields of action where denial of individual or collective dimensions can radically alter the nature of the policy which is pursued. We might approach the problem of unemployment by focusing on the training and capacity of the unemployed person; but we might also seek to respond by expanding the range of activity in the productive economy. We can try to tackle the problem of obesity by focusing on individual behaviour, for example, by educating people about the consequences of their dietary choices, or persuading them to exercise more (both are questionably effective); sometimes we divert arguments about physical exercise into competitive sport, which has only a very weak relationship to physical exercise,[24] and hardly any to the pattern of obesity; or we might intervene in the production and distribution of foodstuffs to ensure that firms do not adulterate food products with sugar.

Rae refers to policies that are concerned with a subclass or category of society as 'bloc-regarding':[25] women, people with disabilities, consumers or any of the other categories I have been considering in this chapter are responded to as if they were a collective group. (Blocs are also sometimes referred to as 'segments' or slices of society, but Rae tries to reserve that term for distinctions within blocs – for example, treating children as a bloc, but then looking at inequalities between children.) Policies addressed to social relationships and structures, such as those dealing with race, gender and class, are collective in methodological terms. Those examples are all 'structural' – they all relate to relationships of power and disadvantage – but there are other social categories which might equally be the focus of collective policy: examples might be policies for children; lone parents; migrants; older people; young people not in education, training or employment; and many others.

Box 2.2: Public transport

Commuting to work is done for a collective purpose, but for the most part, when people commute they do not do it collectively. There is no group decision, but a series of individual decisions with a myriad number of destinations and possible outcomes. Wright and Rogers apply one of the standard methods of individualist methodology, game theory, to make a case for collective action in this field. The problem is that 'rational' individuals seeking to maximise their own benefit will choose private transportation for themselves while preferring others to use public transportation; but if everyone makes the same decision, everyone would use private transportation, and that is the worst combination for everyone. (That, they suggest, is more or less what has happened in the USA.)[26]

If the regulation and provision of transport is 'collective', it is because groups of travellers – commuters, passengers, tourists, business travellers and so on – are

---

[24] See Scottish Health Survey 2008, www.scotland.gov.uk/Publications/2009/09/28102003/68, last obtained 28 September 2018.

[25] D Rae, 1981, *Equalities*, Cambridge, MA: Harvard University Press, ch 2.2.

[26] E Wright, J Rogers, 2015, *American society*, New York: Norton, ch 6.

treated as if they are groups. Part of the reason for that is the sheer number of people who have to be considered. The London Underground carries 1.37 billion passengers a year; Waterloo Station alone serves over 100 million passengers in a year.[27] Dealing with thousands of people every hour is not like dealing with a handful of people, and simply multiplying up; as the numbers grow, the experience of each person has to take into account the presence of the others. Thought has to be given to services, flows and contingencies – coping with every possible eventuality, because any system exposed to billions of iterations will experience whatever is possible in due course. Assessments of public policy in this field are often made on the basis of cost-benefit analysis, an individualistic attempt to compare the position of those who gain and those who lose from such developments. This process suffers from the central problem that people's circumstances are intertwined with everyone else's, and very small fluctuations in the valuation of personal gains or losses (such as travel time) have very large cumulative effects on the outcomes of the analysis. And so an issue like the management of transport is dealt with collectively, not in the sense that everyone is treated as having the same objectives, but because every possible objective is liable to be shared with others.

Public transport is part of a complex constellation of regulation and management of movement. The basic rationale for providing transport for bunches of people is, first, that people share common destinations; second, that concentrating them in particular modes of transport improves conditions for others, while failing to do so imposes costs; third, that certain forms of rapid transport (such as a metro system) become feasible despite the numbers of people involved. Tyson argues that the basic tests are efficiency, externalities (the implications for other people) and land use.[28] Where there is no public transport, there are implicit costs: either people have to live closer to their destinations, which usually has implications for population density, housing design and public space, or if they use individual transport, there has to be system capable of coping with large numbers. Public transportation is treated as a collective problem because an individualised approach is impractical.

Box 2.2 focuses on public transport, a classic example where people are treated as a bloc, rather than attempting to respond to their

27 Transport for London, 2018, Facts and figures, https://tfl.gov.uk/corporate/about-tfl/what-we-do/london-underground/facts-and-figures, last obtained 28 September 2018.
28 W Tyson, 1976, Transport and planning: the rationale of public transport subsidies, *Town Planning Review* 47 (4) 315–24.

circumstances individually. Like other examples given previously in this section, it emphasises not just the potential to treat people as if they were a group, but the possibility that this may offer genuinely different ways of approaching problems that might otherwise be constructed at the individual level. It is possible to distinguish societal policies – bloc-regarding policies that are concerned with whole categories – from policies that are specifically intended to treat people in groups. Table 2.1 points to a few examples. The examples represent alternative approaches, but none of them is exclusive; in most cases there are different ways of tackling the same issues, and often people will argue for all of them simultaneously.

In terms of the historical development of services, most of the provision in the third column of the table preceded the kinds of policy that are outlined in the second. Collective and group provision has mainly been the province of civil society, whereas the 'social responses' identified here have typically been carried out by governments. Civil society is often thought of, by the individualists of the New Right, as if it were based in interactions between individuals; but, looked at dispassionately, some of the longest-established social institutions, such as schools and hospitals, function on a collective social basis. There are individuated alternatives, but they are less common than the collective options.

Table 2.1: Individuated, collective and structural policies

	Individuated responses	Social/structural responses	Collective/group provision
Poverty	Means testing	Universality	Mutualised pension funds
Health	Dietary advice	Taxing and restricting harmful substances, such as tobacco	Public hospitals
Children	Substitute family care	Banning corporal punishment	Schools
People with disabilities	Aids and adaptations	Rules about accessibility	Residential care

3

Moral collectivism

The morality of collective action

There is no universally accepted view of moral conduct, and there are many shades of moral opinion, but for the purposes of explanation and discussion it can be taken in lumps. There are four main types of moral judgment: consequentialism, universal principles, particularism and virtue ethics.

Consequentialist morality depends on the idea that moral actions are supposed to benefit people, or at least that they are intended to do so. In collectivist terms, it implies that collective organisations should try to promote the common good. They should try to stop bad things happening – things to be avoided, or things that work to everyone's detriment, such as war or pollution. The idea of a common good and shared interests is basic to many visions of society – the 'harmony' of Robert Owen, the idea of a common weal, or the simple economics that judges human development through a series of indicators such as the Gross Domestic Product.

People do have interests in common. Some of those interests are human – we all need to eat, to have shelter and so forth; some are things we have learned to rely on, such as beds, telephones or refrigerators – the degree of consensus about 'essential' items is striking; others are communal, such as a shared interest in a clean environment or common use of communal facilities like roads, power supplies or urban infrastructure. Many patterns of behaviour are common, because they are socialised. Old people have diverse experiences, but by virtue of their age they share concerns about, for example, policies for retirement, pensions and the maintenance of health. Children require education, material stability and emotional support. Everyone is first a child, and most of us expect to become old; these concerns are likely to affect all of us in some way. Pensions, schooling and medical care are not universal truths of human nature; they are methods that have developed to make people's lives better. Some societies aim to eradicate certain undesirable options: if in Britain we no longer have houses with no running water or sanitation, it is because of regulation and compulsory acquisition and demolition. The ways in which the problems are defined, and policies are formed to deal with them, depend on the society in which they occur. People may differ in their choices, or in their views as to how these issues are best dealt with, but the interests apply to very large numbers of people, and through them to every member of a society. (I return to the issue of the common good in Chapter 9.)

The second class of moral norms depends on universal principles – norms that apply to everyone, in all societies. Universal principles are based in deontological or rule-based obligations: principles that we follow because they are right. Religious rules are often cast in those terms; so are the principles of human rights. The application of universal principles often seems to challenge the position of groups, communities and societies, because groups and societies are based on a complex network of particular obligations, and universal principles cut through them. There is no reason why universal principles should not apply to social groups – a family, a community or a nation. (Many rules of the sort do. In contemporary Western society, we tend to forget that early laws applied to families and heads of household, rather than individuals: so when the Bible tells us not to marry our sons and daughters to certain groups, or to control how our servants behave on the Sabbath,[1] we re-interpret that, against the sense of the words, as an injunction on the individual rather than a rule for a household.) Human rights adhere to each and every person, regardless of the society they live in. Most of those rights, such as the right to a fair trial, to property or to privacy, tend to be seen as the rights of individuals – because if they do not apply at the level of the individual, they do not apply to everyone. But not all human rights are reducible to the rights of individuals. The rights of minority groups are important, too: rights to cultural expression are a significant example. Rights against genocide are among the most important of all human rights, and they have a collective dimension that is not contained solely within the right of individuals to life. It follows that universal principles can be used, not just to condemn groups, but to defend them too.

Particular principles, the third class of morals, are based in the specific obligations that people are subject to because of their relationships to other people. MacIntyre writes:

> we all approach our own circumstances as bearers of a
> particular social identity. I am someone's son or daughter,

---

[1]   Deuteronomy 7:3 and 5:14.

> someone else's cousin or uncle; I am a citizen of this or that
> city, a member of this or that guild or profession; I belong
> to this clan, that tribe, this nation. Hence what is good for
> me has to be the good for one who inhabits these roles.[2]

The particular identities and obligations we have structure our relationships in terms of families, professions, clans, tribes and nations. People are not born into a moral vacuum; they are born into families, communities and countries. That means, for every person, there is a complex, thick set of relationships, norms and obligations, which has to be taken into account in any moral discussion. One of the most serious defects in contemporary individualist thought is the treatment of people as moral voids, entirely motivated by self-interest; few people are like that, and those who are, are treated as having a mental disorder. A discussion of the moral dimensions of collectivism largely then focuses on the moral dimensions of living in society, not to the moral obligations that a person has to the greater good.

There are moral rules for groups, not just rules for individuals. It is tempting to argue that particular rules must be collective in some way, because they can only apply within an existing framework of complementary norms. That is an argument about social norms, rather than collective norms as such. For example, particular rules apply to anyone who makes a contract, and that process might be highly individualised. Some of the rules that might seem at first to be collective, such as provision for pensions in European 'welfare states', often turn out in practice to be based on a series of individual contracts, referring to individualised contributions and entitlements. When a group of Peruvian pensioners took their rights to social security to the Inter-American Human Rights court,[3] they won not because the court thought that everyone ought to have a pension, but because the reduction of their pension was seen as a denial of their property rights.

There is another sense, however, in which collective morality is deeply particularist. The association is there because substantive collectivism depends heavily on the existence of networks of social relationships; it would have little meaning without those relationships. MacIntyre refers to the importance of roles: that understanding, too, is basic to collective action. The way that we recognise the existence

---

[2]   A MacIntyre, 1981, *After virtue*, London: Duckworth.
[3]   Five Pensioners v Peru, cited T Melish, 2008, The Inter American Court on Human Rights, in M Langford (ed) 2008, *Social rights jurisprudence*, Cambridge: Cambridge University Press, pp 387, 398–400.

of a social group, and the way that we identify obligations between people, are essentially and fundamentally the same. Indeed, one of the characteristic elements of social groups is that there must be some means of identifying the relationships between its members, and those relationships are communal in their nature.

The fourth category of moral principle, virtue ethics, identifies the morality of actions by considering what a good person would do in the circumstances. The virtues include, for example, honesty, integrity and consideration. That may seem vague, but rules cannot cover every situation, and moral dilemmas happen in the areas of uncertainty: the virtues are the sort of morality that parents attempt to teach their children, so that they will have some idea how to approach moral problems. Virtuous conduct is a matter of disposition, consideration, discussion and awareness, not simply of following preset rules. There can be virtuous collectives, or at least it can be argued that collectives should try to become progressively more virtuous than before. Lawton and his colleagues point to four key elements of moral conduct: moral sensitivity, the exercise of moral reasoning or judgment, moral motivation (the place accorded to moral values) and moral character.[4] Ethical conduct does not ask people to anticipate every possible eventuality, or every possible rule that might apply; it is a matter of disposition and approach.

The recommendations and approaches of different moral positions overlap, but they lead in different directions. Particularism depends on the social context. Consequentialism calls for moral judgments to be made when we know what the outcomes are. Virtue ethics makes allowances for human failings. Universal principles apply to every case, regardless of what happens next.

Groups as moral actors

Moral individualism is based on the rights and responsibilities of individuals;[5] moral collectivism emphasises the rights and responsibilities of groups. Moral collectivism has its roots in the idea that a group can be a moral actor – making decisions on ethical grounds, and being judged for its conduct as a moral agent.[6] This kind of argument begins

---

[4]   A Lawton, J Rayner, K Lasthuizen, 2012, *Ethics and management in the public sector*, London: Routledge, pp 16, 124.

[5]   See P Spicker, 2013, *Reclaiming individualism*, Bristol: Policy Press, ch 3.

[6]   See e.g. P Pettit, 2007, Responsibility Incorporated, *Ethics* 117 170–20; S Collins, H Lawford-Smith, 2015, Collectives' and individuals' obligations, *Canadian Journal of Philosophy* 46 (1) 38–58.

with an acceptance of collectivism as a meaningful set of relationships – if collective entities did not exist, as some individualists assert, only individuals could be responsible for moral conduct. But there is some inconsistency in the reductive position: individualists commonly focus on a conflict between individualism and collectivism, and that conflict cannot happen unless collectives also have a moral status. Accepting that groups have a moral status – that they are not simply the passive object of moral consideration, but engaged in moral action and behaviour – has the direct implication that groups, too, are subject to moral judgment and reasoning.

The simplest form of engagement is clear when groups enter into obligations. It should not be difficult to accept that groups can do this – it happens all the time. For example, it is possible for a business to make a contract. 'Businesses' are not all alike. Some businesses are single-handed operators; some are based on partnerships, where the partners accept responsibility jointly and severally; but most business of any size is something different again. Any 'limited company' – that is, a company with limited liability in the event of its failure – is corporate, which means that it has an existence which is distinct from its owners. An electricity company, a volume builder, a bank or a telecoms provider do not make contracts between the senior partners, the managers or the shareholders and the public; they make contracts in their own right. Firms can be bought and sold. They can buy and sell other firms. Much of the world's wealth is held by corporations, not by individuals. Bankruptcy, when it happens, is often bankruptcy of the firm, not of the participants. And a contract, in its nature, involves undertaking an obligation – typically of payment for goods or services rendered.

Moral engagement goes beyond promises and undertakings. Many legal jurisdictions define corporations as 'juridical persons'; they treat them as if they were individual persons in law, so that they can behave as if they were human beings, able to make agreements, to instigate legal action or even to face criminal charges. Organisations, like individuals, can act immorally, cheat, defraud or kill people. Not all legal systems recognise all of those points, but many do. Sometimes the restrictions on corporate prosecution seem arbitrary: for example, businesses in UK law cannot be convicted of corporate theft as such, despite the obvious fact that a business can wrongly appropriate someone else's property, but they can be convicted of false accounting or 'dishonestly retaining a wrongful credit' (which, of course, depends on the premise that businesses can act dishonestly). Some legal systems have special status for organisations of different stamps, each with defined roles and status.

Examples are trades unions, religious bodies and cooperatives. We expect organisations to behave morally: to be trustworthy, responsive and respectful of others.

There are those who reduce the moral character of an organisation to the moral character to the individuals who make it up.[7] Isaacs reviews several objections to collective moral responsibility, finding all of them wanting. They are that:

- collective responsibility holds people responsible for the actions of others;
- it requires the punishment of innocent individuals;
- it precludes individual moral responsibility;
- it reifies social structures;
- because collectives lack consciousness they cannot be responsible; and
- everything is reducible to the actions of individuals.[8]

The first three objections stem from a common confusion. Holding a group responsible is not the same thing as holding its members individually responsible; nor does blame attaching to one exonerate the other. Imagine that a social security agency sets out grounds for review which are scrupulously followed by its employees, but there are so many problems to review that the organisation is unable to process the results timeously, and claimants suffer hardship.[9] The fault is a fault of procedure; the moral failing is the failing of the organisation, not of the officers who are referring cases for review. Conversely, suppose that while a hospital management board is focused on improving service efficiency, an old person in one of its beds is dying for want of a glass of water.[10] That might be blamed on the organisation[11] – or treated as failure of 'leadership', whatever that is[12] – but it is also a failure of the

---

[7] M Velasquez, 2003, Debunking corporate moral responsibility, *Business Ethics Quarterly* 13 (4) 531–62.

[8] T Isaacs, 2011, *Moral responsibility in collective contexts*, Oxford: Oxford University Press, pp 59–60.

[9] Social Security Advisory Committee, 2016, *Decision making and mandatory reconsideration*, London: SSAC.

[10] *Daily Mail*, 2010, Patients at scandal-hit hospital 'forced to drink from vases after being left on ward without water', www.dailymail.co.uk/news/article-1332070/Stafford-Hospital-inquiry-Patients-left-water-forced-drink-vases.html, last obtained 28 September 2018.

[11] R Francis (chair) 2013, *Report of the Mid Staffordshire NHS Foundation Trust Public Inquiry*, HC 898-1, London: TSO.

[12] P Spicker, 2012, 'Leadership': a perniciously vague concept, *International Journal of Public Sector Management* 25 (1) 34–47.

individual nurses and staff members responsible for that patient's care. It does not follow, from any demonstration that individuals have moral responsibility for things that a group has done, that the group has none. Proof that a group is at fault is not proof either that individuals in it are at fault, or that they are not. There is a much stronger case for the dualist position, that while people in groups have to be responsible for their actions individually, the group may also bear responsibility in its own right. If collective moral responsibility coexists with individual responsibility, then questions of how moral failings should be addressed need to be considered from both perspectives.

The other three objections are more or less equivalent to the claim that everything is reducible to individuals; they are used to deny everything social, as if laws, government or organisations had no meaning. There are those who believe that corporate actions must ultimately be the judgments of individuals, because they have 'no souls to damn, and no bodies to kick',[13] and those who simply pass them over. Corporations may not have bodies, but the law treats them as if they did – the idea is built in to the meaning of 'incorporation'. Many critics complain about 'reification' – treating social relationships and constructs as if they were things. It seems that, by this account, collective entities have no identity, relationships, processes or procedures in their own right. I have to assume that the people who think this do not work for an organisation, have not been to school or university, have no bank account, have never applied for a passport or a driving licence and have never sat in a committee meeting. Denying the existence of social relationships and constructs is pretty much on a level with Bishop Berkeley's assertion that we cannot prove other human beings exist[14] – maybe we cannot, but where does that leave us?

There may well be limits to the moral responsibility of groups, as there are limits to the moral responsibility of individuals. Hedahl argues that some organisations lack the capacity to make moral judgments that individuals within the organisation might make.[15] That is sometimes true; for example, the constitution of many charities prevents them from diverting resources to pressing needs.

---

[13] Cited Isaacs, 2011, p 63.

[14] G Berkeley, 1713, Three dialogues, in *A new theory of vision and other writings*, London: Dent, 1910.

[15] M Hedahl, 2013, The collective fallacy, *Philosophy of the Social Sciences* 43 (3) 283–300.

But the issue is not just that individuals can make different judgments from groups; it is that there are often different criteria applying to organisations, which means that at times organisations act badly when no individual is at fault, and vice versa. Recently, there has been some reaction against the unthinking dominance of individualism in this field, and writers have sought to justify the common-sense perception that maybe businesses, charities, institutions and so forth do have a social existence.[16]

Box 3.1 outlines the sorts of considerations that need to be taken into account by a public service that aims to act ethically. Much of what defines an ethical institution is not so much its moral purpose, as a set of processes and standards that will ensure that decisions and actions are guided by ethical principles and respect ethical constraints. In the voluntary sector, there are many organisations with charitable objectives that follow strict rules of governance. For a charity, the rules will usually be laid out in a foundation document, or a constitution – the principle that a charity should be governed in accordance with the wishes of its founders has been applied for more than a thousand years.[17] A modern charitable constitution will usually include the charitable objectives, relationships with participants and beneficiaries and processes linked to public accountability.

Prescriptions for good conduct in organisations do at times read, to their detriment, like ancient tablets of stone. The Nolan Principles, which almost all people newly appointed to public service in the UK are expected to affirm, are a prime example: they include Selflessness; Integrity; Objectivity; Accountability; Openness; Honesty and Leadership.[18] Some gaps are unavoidable, but there is nothing in these principles that would have safeguarded agencies and the people they serve from some of the worst abuses in recent years – cases which show not so much a lack of probity as incompetence, neglect of duty and a callous disregard for human dignity.[19]

---

[16] e.g. C List, P Pettit, 2011, *Group agency*, Oxford: Oxford University Press; Isaacs, 2011.

[17] J Brodman, 2009, *Charity and religion in medieval Europe*, Washington, DC: Catholic University of America Press.

[18] Cm 2850, Committee on Standards in Public Life (chair: Lord Nolan), 1995, *Standards in Public Life*, London: TSO.

[19] P Spicker, 2014, Seven principles of public life: time to rethink, *Public Money and Management* 34 (1) 11–18.

Box 3.1: Ethical conduct in the public services

When people become part of a social organisation, and act collectively within it, they are not necessarily functioning as independent human beings. Indeed, some of the things that independent human beings might reasonably do – favouring their children, protecting their personal interests, losing their temper – are disapproved of, and considered improper or even unethical. The Nolan Principles ask public officials to be 'selfless'.[20] The central principle is that individual behaviour is subordinated to the organisational role – and so, that the ethical requirements of that role take over. Some organisational roles are professional, and the people in them are ethically accountable to external professional bodies. Some are bureaucratic; in a bureaucracy, Weber tells us, 'the regular activities required for the purposes of the bureaucratically governed structure are distributed in a fixed way as official duties'.[21] Some are based in other conventions of management, including 'leadership' and compliance with instructions.

In general terms, there are four main categories of principle to consider. First, there is the relationship of the agency to the people it serves – its clients, service users or the general public. Service users often have rights to a service, and services often have a duty to respond to need. Officials need not to take advantage of vulnerable service users, for example, by demanding bribes or favours.

The second set of rules governs the relationship between the agency and the system of legitimate public authority. Part of this will be a consideration of the source of the authority. In the case of government agencies, this will be the delegation of authority from a constitution or sovereign authority; for charities, it will relate to a foundation document or constitution.

Third, there is the conduct of the administration. The rules of 'natural justice' guarantee a hearing;[22] there needs to be some system for dealing with complaints and mistakes, such as a system for review or appeal. There is usually a duty to be fair, which implies that similar cases should be treated in similar ways, but that principle is subject to lots of others; in social work, for example, rather more emphasis is put on the identification of risk or potential harm, and consistency is a secondary principle which can be difficult to judge.

---

[20] Cm 2850, 1995.

[21] M Weber (1921), in H H Gerth, C Wright Mills, 1948, *From Max Weber*, London: RKP, p 195.

[22] W Wade, C Forsyth, 2000, *Administrative law*, Oxford: Oxford University Press, 8th edition.

Fourth, there is the relationship of officials to the agency. These rules typically cover such issues as probity (for example, not taking bribes), integrity and selflessness. Corruption, a major problem in many developing countries and transitional economies, typically happens when officials are given opportunities to advance their own interests without being checked.[23]

It is debatable whether moral action by individual participants is enough to guarantee the morality of the collective organisation – an army can be staffed by competent, ethically engaged soldiers, and still do terrible things. It is at least plausible, however, to suggest that a collective organisation is less likely to do things which are immoral if the people in it are guided by ethical considerations, and conversely that it is more likely to do things which are immoral if the people in it disregard ethical norms. Ethical guidelines cannot predict every eventuality, but they are an important safeguard.

Extending this type of ethical standard to other types of social group can be difficult, because other groups are not often backed up by the same kind of structures. It has been argued that group responsibility can be attributed to 'random collectives', people who happen to be in the same place at the same time, if only they can be taken to have a possibility of being 'minimally organized' as a group.[24] I do not think that is very helpful for understanding how collectives work, but have to recognise that some legal positions (for example, public order offences such as riot) work on a similar principle. Some people talk about families and communities as if they were like businesses, but they do not have the same structures or rights – a family cannot make a contract, and a community would have to set up a legal organisation to do so. (That seems odd, because families and communities represent much older, longer established types of legal relationships than corporate businesses do. The oddness has been recognised in some of the literature on family law. Shaffer argues for a view of 'the family as organic and as prior to individuality', and argues that in families, it is the family – not the individuals in it – which creates promises, contracts and consent in

[23]   W Savedoff, K Hussmann, 2006, Why are health systems prone to corruption?, in Transparency International, *Global corruption report 2006*, https://www.transparency. org/whatwedo/publication/global_corruption_report_2006_corruption_and_ health, last obtained 28 September 2018.

[24]   R Manning, 1985, The random collective as a moral agent, *Social Theory and Practice* 11 (1) 97–105.

the domestic sphere. The imposition of radical individualism on family affairs, he writes, is 'sad, corrupting and untruthful.'[25])

At root, the argument that groups can be moral actors follows from one of the central precepts of substantive collectivism. All social groups have an identity and a capacity for common action: those are aspects of what makes them a group. Wherever common action takes place, it may be subject to moral criteria and considered from a moral perspective. The mutual support that people give each other in families or communities is usually thought of as a good thing, but it is open to an observer to think that forced marriages to preserve a family's honour are a bad thing. Promoting a community's culture is usually seen as a good thing, but ethnic conflict might reasonably be thought of as a bad thing – an example of group behaviour that invites moral condemnation.

There are individualists who would deny that these examples can be thought of as actions by groups. Some people have been sceptical about the idea that any conflict can be usefully described as ethnic, arguing that relating wars to ethnicity or tribal identity masks a huge range of different motivations.[26] This defence was raised in the Rwandan genocide. It was claimed that the violence was spontaneously generated. If it was true, the argument went, there was no collective action, and there could not have been a genocide.[27] The International Criminal Tribunal found, on the contrary, that attacks had been planned, organised and conducted by identifiable actors and groups.[28] Ethnic conflict does happen, and 'ethnic cleansing' is a demonstration of it; people can be systematically persecuted, attacked and murdered because they belong to a distinct social group. Both the reason for crime, and its moral importance, need to be understood in collective perspective.

Collectivism is sometimes understood as a position which gives priority to collective goals and interests over the interests of individuals.[29] (That identification helps to explain the otherwise puzzling confusion

---

[25] T Shaffer, 1987, The legal ethics of radical individualism, Notre Dame Law School, http://scholarship.law.nd.edu/law_faculty_scholarship/533, last obtained 28 September 2018.

[26] B Gilley, 2004, Against the concept of ethnic conflict, *Third World Quarterly* 25 (6) 1155–66.

[27] M Ngoga, 2010, Why we're prosecuting Peter Erlinder, *Guardian*, https://www.theguardian.com/law/2010/jul/03/why-prosecute-peter-erlinder, last obtained 28 September 2018.

[28] United Nations, 2015, Mechanism for International Criminal Tribunals: Legacy website of the International Criminal Tribunal for Rwanda, http://unictr.unmict.org/en/tribunal, last obtained 28 September 2018.

[29] M Brewer, Y Chen, 2007, Where (who) are collectives in collectivism?, *Psychological Review* 141 (1) 133–51, p 137.

between holism and collectivism: if holism is a view that collectives supervene on individual actions in practice, collectivism becomes the disposition or moral justification that legitimates the priority.) Implicitly this suggests that collective goals are being valued above individual ones. I will be discussing the relationship between individuals and collectives further in the following chapter, but there is an obvious problem in characterising collectivism morally in these terms. Whatever the moral framework that people apply, it has to be true that collective groups can do good things or bad ones. Any moral priority has to be contingent on what is actually being done, and how.

That point may seem obvious to the point of being trivial, but it stands against two doctrines that attempt to settle the moral questions simply by excluding the opposing position from moral consideration. One problem relates to forms of collectivism that disregard individuals altogether, of the sort favoured by Hegelians and fascists: the collectivity (and in particular the state) is motivated by higher reasoning, God or History (with a capital 'H'). The other comes from unbridled individualism: if only individuals can make moral decisions, anything good or bad has to be attributable to them. This may look, at first sight, as if it places the moral burden squarely on individuals, but it has a catastrophic side effect: it excuses the same individuals from the wrongful actions of the group, because if they are not acting immorally themselves, the immorality must be attributable to someone else.[30] So we find, as a corollary of this argument, that often large organisations in liberal societies are able to bully,[31] conceal,[32] defraud[33] and intimidate,[34] and no one is responsible. Too often, industrial corporations are treated as if they were beyond good and evil.

---

[30] P French, 1984, *Collective and corporate responsibility*, New York: Columbia University Press, pp x–xi.

[31] A Monaghan, S Butler, 2014, Small businesses facing bullying by corporate customers, *Guardian*, https://www.theguardian.com/business/2014/dec/11/small-businesses-facing-bullying-corporate-customers, last obtained 28 September 2018.

[32] A Palin, 2013, How managers conceal the profits of price fixing, *Financial Times* https://www.ft.com/content/7e92698a-bd63-11e2-890a-00144feab7de, last obtained 28 September 2018.

[33] B Maclean, 2017, How Wells Fargo's cutthroat corporate culture allegedly drove bankers to fraud, *Vanity Fair*, https://www.vanityfair.com/news/2017/05/wells-fargo-corporate-culture-fraud, last obtained 28 September 2018.

[34] E Bloxham, 2014, A lazy, expensive way to intimidate shareholders, Fortune, http://fortune.com/2014/03/14/a-lazy-expensive-way-to-intimidate-shareholders, last obtained 28 September 2018.

Reconciling moral collectivism with moral individualism

Individualism and collectivism are often constructed as belief systems or ideologies, mutually contradictory, mutually exclusive. At one extreme, individualism appears to be a gospel of moral selfishness – the philosophy of Ayn Rand or the (fictional) Gordon Gekko in *Wall Street*. The laissez-faire of the 19th century brought prosperity to some, and poverty and human misery to others. At the other extreme, collectivism appears as a doctrine that wholly suppresses individuality in the belief that the group is the superior moral force. One of the reasons why individualism is stated so forcefully by writers such as Popper[35] or Hayek[36] is that they had come to associate collective morality with the abuses of totalitarian societies.

For Michael Oakeshott, collectivism implies 'an understanding of government in which its proper office is believed to be the imposition upon its subjects of a single pattern of government'.[37] I think he is mistaken – there are many varieties of collectivism, as Oakeshott himself recognises – but there is a case to answer. In the course of the last century, remorseless collectivists, guided by patriotism, communism or fascism, sent millions of people to their deaths. Box 3.2 says more.

Box 3.2: Fascism: the dark side of moral collectivism

There are moral dangers in collectivism – the problem that emphasising community values poses to individuals who want to be different, or the danger that an idea of the common good might suppress the concerns of minorities. There have been much worse cases, and the extreme is most clearly represented in fascism. Fascism is an approach to politics, particularly associated with authoritarian and racist movements in Italy, Germany and Spain in the 1930s and '40s. The Marxist opposition of the time was baffled by fascism, and it was for a long time the received wisdom in academic circles to argue either that fascism was another avenue of capitalist exploitation, or that fascism was incoherent and meaningless. It is true that fascism was different in different places – in Spain, it was more plainly a label put on conservative militarism – but the same kind of accusation could be

---

[35] K Popper, 1945, *The open society and its enemies*, vol 2, London: Routledge and Kegan Paul.

[36] F Hayek, 1948, *Individualism and economic order*, Chicago, IL: University of Chicago Press.

[37] M Oakeshott, 1993, *Morality and politics in modern Europe*, New Haven, CT: Yale University Press.

levelled at any political ideology in practice. We could with equal justice argue that there is no coherent or unitary understanding of conservatism, or socialism, or liberalism, and those criticisms would miss the point just as thoroughly. Though it appealed to long traditions of authoritarian nationalism, fascism presented an explicit, prominent and emotionally powerful ideology.

Fascism elevated the state and the nation above the individual: in Mussolini's phrase, 'everything for the state, nothing outside the state, nothing against the state'. Fascist ideology begins from two precepts. The first is an authoritarian collectivism. The individual is meaningless; it is the collectivity (the state, the nation or the race) which is paramount. This means that the wishes and actions of each person are necessarily subject to the whole. Paxton, while denying the ideological nature of fascism, notes:

> At its fullest development, fascism redrew the frontiers between private and public ... It changed the practice of citizenship from the enjoyment of constitutional rights and duties to participation in mass ceremonies of affirmation and conformity. It reconfigured relations between the individual and the collectivity, so that an individual had no rights outside community interest. It expanded the powers of the executive – party and state – in a bid for total control.[38]

Neumann identified two organising principles:

> National Socialism takes all organizations under its wing and turns them into official administrative agencies. The pluralistic principle is replaced by a monistic, total, authoritarian organisation. This is the first principle of National Socialist social organization. The second principle is the atomization of the individual. Such groups as the family and the church, the solidarity arising from common work in plants, shops and offices are deliberately broken down.[39]

Neumann's work is an impassioned condemnation of the Nazi state, and his passion may have led to some exaggeration; but if he is right, this model of fascism is based in the suppression of social groups as well as individuals, and that stands in opposition to everything about collectivism that this book is engaged with.

The second aspect is organic corporatism. Fascism was corporatist, in the literal sense where a society or a nation is seen as a body, with government at the

---

[38] R Paxton, 2004, *The anatomy of fascism*, Harmondsworth: Penguin, p 11.
[39] F Neumann, 1942, *Behemoth: The structure and practice of National Socialism*, London: Gollancz, p 326.

head. It is 'organic' in the sense that the body politic is a complex organism, like any biological entity. States or nations have a collective will, and a distinct existence. The image of the body is an important one, frequently used by fascists to justify their actions. (Golden Dawn, in Greece, has been using similar language.) People who were not part of the nation were like parasites, or lice, on the body. Killing Jews, Himmler said, was a matter of 'cleanliness'. In England, the 'idealist' F H Bradley represented the punishment of crime in terms of Darwinian 'social surgery' – cutting out diseased parts of the nation.

> To remove the innocent is unjust, but it is not, perhaps, in all cases wrong. Their removal, on the contrary, will be right if the general welfare demands it. ... where the good of the whole may call for moral surgery, mere innocence is certainly no exemption or safeguard.[40]

Fascist social policy was built on nationalism and nationhood. In a positive mode, national pride was channelled through cultural propaganda, such as the German emphasis on its musical tradition. Particular emphasis was given to education of young people. The Nazis introduced the Hitler Youth, their own version of the Scout movement, and programmes of 'Strength through Joy' and 'Faith and Beauty' (the latter being for girls). Traditional fairy tales were rewritten, and children's stories about war and heroism were commissioned for the over-nines. Religious education in schools was gradually suspended. More than five million children passed through Strength through Joy.

Family policy was natalist (encouraging births): couples were given loans to marry, subsidies were introduced for children in low-income families and prolific mothers were given medals. 'Good' births were encouraged through a combination of social pressure and incentives: civil servants were pressed to marry and have children, the births of children of SS personnel were paid for, and the 'Lebensborn' programme encouraged racially appropriate breeding.

The converse of this was a set of measures intended to discourage the 'wrong' sort of breeding. Public health was interpreted fundamentally as a racial issue: since the race was represented as a biological entity, it was also considered important to safeguard the biological integrity of the race. This included measures to avoid racial mixing: the Nazi laws on miscegenation (or 'racial defilement') are illustrative. Weindling describes the racial policy as 'a means of social control and of promoting social integration in terms of both ideology and everyday

---

[40] F Bradley, 1894, Some remarks on punishment, in *Collected essays*, Oxford: Clarendon press, 1935, pp 152–3.

habits'.[41] To discourage impure breeding, The Nazis began with sterilisation of the 'genetically unfit'. Grunberger writes: 'By the outbreak of the war, 375,000 people (including 200,000 feeble minded, 73,000 schizophrenics, 57,000 epileptics and nearly 30,000 alcoholics) had been sterilised, the vast majority of them involuntarily.'[42] Ultimately the mechanisms for dealing with the 'defective' were used more extensively; the programme was linked in with medical killing – which Weindling describes as 'a pilot scheme for the holocaust'.[43]

Fascist ideology did not emerge out of nothing during the twentieth century; it drew on a number of political and intellectual sources for its strength. The ideology draws on five key elements in European thought. Hegelian idealism represented the conflict of states as 'the march of God on earth'. Romanticism emphasised the state of mind of heroic individuals and a sensibility to creative art. Nationalism squared both with the ideas of the nation as a thinking, acting, self-determining body and the idealist view of nations as a representation of God's creation; so did the fourth element, the emphasis on racialism and racial purity. Finally, perhaps paradoxically, fascism appealed to people's desire for order and security; the corporatist image encouraged people to put their faith in government and strong leadership. The Pétain government in France sought to replace 'liberty, equality and fraternity' with another slogan: *travail, famille, patrie*, meaning 'work, family and country'. This is not an argument against those principles; it is evidence of the ways that widely held values can be turned to evil purposes.

For Hayek, collective morality consisted of the imposition of a single ethical principle, overriding individual morality:

> From the two central features of every collectivist system, the need for a commonly accepted system of ends of the group, and the all-overriding desire to give to the group the maximum of power to achieve these ends, grows a definite system of morals, which on some points coincides and on others violently contrasts with ours-but differs from it in one point which makes it doubtful whether we can call it morals: that it does not leave the individual conscience free to apply its own rules and does not even know any general rules which the individual is required or allowed to

---

[41] P Weindling, 1989, *Health, race and German politics between national unification and Nazism, 1870–1945*, Cambridge: Cambridge University Press, p 493.

[42] R Grunberger, 1974, *A social history of the Third Reich*, Harmondsworth: Penguin, p 288.

[43] Weindling, 1989, p 548.

observe in all circumstances. This makes collectivist morals so different from what we have known as morals that we find it difficult to discover any principle in them, which they nevertheless possess.[44]

There are genuine problems to address, but there are two sorts of confusion in this critique. The first is that a strongly individualistic moral position does not invalidate substantive statements about group action – on the contrary, much of the appeal of moral individualism rests in its power to oppose the immoral actions of collective bodies. The second is that recognising collective responsibility does not negate individual responsibility – they are not mutually exclusive. There is no intrinsic contradiction in holding that individuals in a substantively collective unit, such as an army, are still morally responsible for their actions; there is no inconsistency in holding that a public agency is morally responsible for a failure in service, but that individual officers have acted as they should have done; and there is no difficulty in attaching moral responsibility to groups and to individuals at the same time.

Individualism and collectivism are often represented as polar opposites. Before it is possible to see them in this light, however, there are a few steps that need to be filled in. The first step is to accept that these are normative positions, not just descriptive ones. There are substantive individualists who deny that collectivism represents any kind of reality, and substantive collectivists who argue that individuality is a social construct, but there is a wide spectrum of opinion; if the argument was genuinely and solely about substantive issues, few people would locate themselves at the extremes. In moral terms, by contrast, opinions are often polarised. It does not matter whether individualism and collectivism exist in a pure, ideal form, or not; it is still possible to base a moral argument on a non-existent ideal.

The next step is to identify what it is about individualism and collectivism that associates them with different moral positions. Beginning with a substantive argument – that this is the way the world is – is not equivalent to saying that this is the way that the world ought to be. There has to be something about either view that is, in itself, of moral value. In the case of individualism, that value is usually the intrinsic value of a human being, expressed in terms of dignity, respect for persons, and rights.[45] In the case of collectivism, the position is

---

[44]   F Hayek, 1944, *The road to serfdom*, London: Routledge, p 150.
[45]   P Spicker, 2013, ch 2.

more complex. There are doctrines (such as patriotism) which assert the intrinsic value of the group in the same way as individualists assert the value of a human being, but that is not the commonest form of collectivism. The argument for a collective approach is as likely to be based on the value, not of the group as such, but of the process of being in a group – identity, mutuality, collaboration, participation and solidarity. Collective values are discussed further in Chapter 8.

The third step requires individualism and collectivism to appear in opposition to each other, so that there is a choice to be made between them. Individualism and collectivism are presented as polar opposites. For the opposition of individualism and collectivism to make sense, there has to be some reason to reject the alternative – if there is not, the two positions could be held at the same time. This is usually done by the argument that while individualism or collectivism is good, there is something about the opposite value that prevents the primary value from being realised. On one hand, group action is seen as suppressing the distinctive individuality, freedom and choice of the individual. On the other, individual self-interest is represented as undermining the cooperation and collaboration that is fundamental to collective action.

The psychological literature suggests that people in different cultures have different dispositions towards collective behaviour. Hofstede points to 'cultures in which people from birth onwards are integrated into strong, cohesive in-groups, often extended families (with uncles, aunts and grandparents) that continue protecting them in exchange for unquestioning loyalty, and oppose other in-groups'.[46] People within a 'collectivist' society are more likely to say 'We' rather than 'I', to stress the importance of belonging to a group, to try to maintain harmony within that group or to accept the values of the group as the basis for common decisions. This approach has been hugely influential in cross-cultural psychology, and many papers refer to individualism and collectivism in these terms – understanding them as opposing moral dispositions. For example, Ball reviews a range of arguments about whether individualist or collectivist norms can be said to lead to economic development, or whether economic development encourages an individualist or collective perspective. Tellingly, there are advocates of every combination.[47]

---

[46] G Hofstede, 2011, Dimensionalizing cultures, *Online Readings in Psychology and Culture* 2 (1), p 11, https://doi.org/10.9707/2307-0919.1014, last obtained 28 September 2018.

[47] R Ball, 2001, Individualism, collectivism and economic development, *Annals of the American Academy of Political and Social Science*, 573 57–84.

There is some reason to question whether this presentation of individualism and collectivism really succeeds in capturing the terms of the debate. Individualism and collectivism are not single, monolithic doctrines, hewn from the rock. In moral discourses, they are principles – ways of approaching the issues. At the beginning of this chapter, I discussed the nature of collectives as moral agents. If they are moral agents, they are capable of doing bad things as well as good things. So any discussion of individualism or collectivism in moral terms moves from being whether individualism or collectivism are good in themselves, to a discussion of how that moral agency should be used. The central moral question for individualists is 'what makes a good person?' The central moral question for collectivists is 'what makes a good society?' Those questions are not mutually exclusive. They are not even opposed.

4

The individual and the collective

Why should individuals join social groups, or accept a role within any collective structure? There are four strong self-interested arguments for acting together with others. The first is the argument for cooperation: people can agree to cooperate for mutual advantage. They may cooperate to increase their wealth, for example, in a partnership. They can cooperate to increase their capacity, because several people can do what the same number of people individually cannot. In economics, there is a 'theory of clubs', concerned primarily with the circumstances where joint action gives people a capacity to obtain resources which they could not get as individuals.[1] The theory is based on a model where there are conflicts about access and congestion and the size of the membership has to be restricted. Buchanan, who developed the idea, offers the simple example of a swimming pool, which would be too expensive for most people to buy from their own resources.[2] However, the same impetus for cooperation and the pooling of resources exists for much larger groups; mutual building societies, which were formed to finance the purchase of housing, are an example.[3]

Cooperation is not usually done by everyone doing the same thing. Typically, it is based on divisions of labour – things are done more effectively when each person in the cooperation has a designated task. The division of labour is basic to economic development, and exchanging goods and labour makes it possible for everyone to get greater resources than they could by relying exclusively on their own efforts as subsistence farmers. Sets of people who agree or act on a division of labour are able to achieve things that individuals in isolation cannot. There is a formal proof of this, the theory of 'comparative advantage' – the idea is drawn from international trade,

---

[1] T Sandler, J Tschirhart, 1997, Club theory: thirty years later, *Public Choice* 93 335–55.

[2] J Buchanan, 1965, An economic theory of clubs, *Economica* 32 (125) 1–14.

[3] E Cleary, 1965, *The Building Society movement*, London: Elek.

but it applies equally within an economy. Even if some people are better at doing everything – an 'absolute advantage' – the effect of specialisation is that they produce more than they could individually. (I would have included the full proof here, but as it demonstrates the reasoning behind cooperation from an individualist perspective, I have already covered it in the earlier book.[4]) People will seek to make arrangements where there is mutual advantage, and those who work together can do more than they could if they tried to do everything themselves.

The second is the argument for mutual support, or the sharing of risks. People can cooperate to share their risks, reducing their vulnerability; individual risks, especially remote risks, are unpredictable and difficult to guard oneself against, but pooling risks with other people stabilises the situation, making adverse conditions and circumstances relatively predictable. That is why people buy insurance; it is also a key reason for the development of public welfare systems. It is possible in principle for insurance to be done only as a transaction between two people, but expanding the range of people who pool their risks adds to the security and level of protection that is being provided. This is the process which led to the growth of social insurance, and ultimately to the welfare states: people joined associations for mutual protection, the associations grew, and in most cases, governments decided to join in after the associations were already a considerable size.[5]

The third argument is pragmatic. Some things are only really possible if several people do them. The sheer practical necessity of organising collective activity leads to the development of structures to do the job. The bodies that own and manage resources like water, energy, telecommunications or food production are already there – well established, well resourced and offering goods at advantageous prices. It can be difficult to start up such activities in countries which have no infrastructure, but once they have started non-participation is a poor option, and ignoring their existence would be perverse. People relate to groups because that is how things are done. Related to that, there is an argument based on the 'new institutional economics', which recognises and interprets decisions through established patterns of collective behaviour. Institutions, North argues, define a structure for economic and social behaviour to take place. Organisations interact, within that structure, do things in particular ways. If things seem to

---

[4]   See P Spicker, 2013, *Reclaiming individualism*, Bristol: Policy Press, pp 151–3.
[5]   P Baldwin, 1990, *The politics of social solidarity*, Cambridge: Cambridge University Press.

work (and sometimes even if they do not work that well), they find it easier not to alter established practice; there is a tendency to 'path dependency'. Over time, conventions are established, and settled practice becomes the norm.[6]

The fourth argument is about the value of collaboration as a process. Collaboration is not only a means to an end; it is also an end in itself. It is a major force in bringing people together, forming social groups, building relationships, developing a sense of community and shared identity.

People's relationship to groups is not necessarily rational or self-interested. The literature on cross-cultural psychology has principally focused on the attitudes which may lead individuals to give priority to group interests over their own, and to do that it tests whether they agree with statements that can be understood as individualist or collectivist in their orientation. A clutch of measures have been devoted to the task: individualism–collectivism,[7] allocentrism versus idiocentrism,[8] the private and the collective self.[9] Brewer and Chen question the validity of many of these measures: in their view, they fail to distinguish collectivist priorities from other kinds of social relationship.[10] There is some empirical support for this distinction: a collectivist orientation can be separated from an emphasis on close personal relations.[11] What that mainly means, however, is that some people, and people in some cultures, define themselves more or less in relation to others, and more or less in terms of their membership of wider social groups. In so far as this is cultural, it is collective rather than individual; individual responses can be used to mark out indicators of cultural behaviour, but agreement or disagreement with attitudinal statements may not be the best test of how people will actually behave collectively. In so far as this is a question of individual decision making, a calculation

[6] D North, 1992, Institutions and economic theory, *The American Economist* 36 (1) 3–6.

[7] D Oyserman, H Coon, M Kemmelmeier, 2002, Rethinking individualism and collectivism, *Psychological Bulletin* 128 (1) 3–72.

[8] H Triandis, 2001, Individualism-collectivism and personality, *Journal of Personality* 6 (1) 907–24.

[9] D Trafimow, H Triandis, S Goto, 1991, Some tests of the distinction between the private self and the collective self, *Journal of Personality and Social Psychology* 60 (5) 649–55.

[10] M Brewer, Y Chen, 2007, Where (who) are collectives in collectivism?, *Psychological Review* 114 (1) 133–51.

[11] Y Kashima, U Kim, M Gelfand, S Yamaguchi, S Choi, M Yuki, 1995, Culture, gender and self, *Journal of Personality and Social Psychology* 69 (5) 925–37.

of self-interest may not come into it. Some individuals may defer to groups because they feel constrained to do so; some may conform out of respect for values encouraging conformity and compliance. More profoundly, there is a degree of 'interdependent self-construal':[12] individuals construct their sense of self and personal identity, at least in part, from their relationships with other people and their position in collective groups.

Ultimately, we do not need to have any special reason to do things in groups. We are born into families, communities, religious and cultural groups; group activity is a normal part of everyday life. People join groups, and become part of groups, because that is the way that people live. The main questions we face are not about whether we should join any groups, but how we should relate to the groups we are part of. Living, sharing, working and doing things together with other people are aspects of what it means to be human.

Individual and group interests

The main individualist objection to collective action is that group interests and group action are incompatible with the recognition of individual interests. All groups, in the view of the most determined individualists, consist of individuals, and only of individuals. The interests of individuals will always diverge from the interests of the group, and consequently self-interested individuals, if they cannot exploit the group, will either refuse to cooperate or defect from the group. Groups can only subsist by repressing individual interests.

The first of these propositions, that all groups consist of individuals, is overstated; it rests on a distortion of perspective. Too much emphasis on consensus and shared interests can certainly lead to the suppression of minority interests and ways of living; but everyone who is part of a group is an individual as well as being a member of the group. 'Individuals', 'groups' and 'society' may decide things in different ways, but these are not terms for different kinds of people. The 'individual' is as much a social construct as the group: real people have a complex set of social relationships, and those relationships routinely include membership of groups, where they will occupy certain roles. When we are talking about employees, or officials, or students, or clients, we are not talking about people as individuals; we are talking about

---

[12] Kashima et al, 1995; S Cross, P Bacon, M Morris, 2004, The relational-interdependent self-construal and relationships, *Journal of Personality and Social Psychology* 78 (4) 791–808.

people occupying particular roles, in particular contexts. We are likely to switch between different modes of discourse depending on the subject we are talking about.

The next stage of the argument claims that the interests of individuals will diverge from the interests of the group. Arrow's 'impossibility theorem' claims to show that it is never possible to identify social preferences from an aggregation of the preferences of individuals.

> It is assumed that each individual in the community has a definite ordering of all conceivable social states in terms of their desirability to him ... The individual may order all social states in terms of their desirability to him. ... If there are at least three alternatives among which the members of society are free to order in any way, then every social welfare function ... must be imposed or dictatorial.[13]

Arrow takes it as axiomatic that individuals will differ. Sen identifies in this a principle of 'universal domain': social preferences must 'yield a social ordering for every possible combination of individual preferences'.[14] Every possible combination? Given a choice between a luxury watch, a pet python and a ton of manure, people have to be expected to rank them diversely in every possible order – regardless, apparently, of benefit, cost, value, circumstances, importance, or even sheer inconvenience. Insisting on the pattern of choices that people are bound to make is designed to force the argument to a predetermined conclusion. Arrow claims that a consensus about preferences can only be achieved through dictatorship.[15] In the UK 97% of households have a washing machine, 95% have central heating and 95% have a mobile phone.[16] This has happened without calling on a dictator to make it happen. The assumption that everyone must have divergent, incompatible preferences is not true; it is not even minimally plausible.

[13] K Arrow, 1950, A difficulty in the concept of social welfare, *Journal of Political Economy* 58(4) 328–346, pp 333, 342.

[14] A Sen, 2000, Rationality and social choice, in R Kuenne (ed) *Readings in social welfare*, Oxford: Blackwell, p 122.

[15] K Arrow, 1967, Values and collective decision making, in E Phelps (ed) *Economic justice*, Harmondsworth: Penguin.

[16] Office for National Statistics 2017, Family Spending in the UK: statistical bulletin, Table A45, https://www.ons.gov.uk/peoplepopulationandcommunity/personalandhouseholdfinances/expenditure/bulletins/familyspendingintheuk/financialyearendingmarch2016, last obtained 29 September 2018.

As individuals always have different interests from the group, the argument runs, any individual would be foolish to join a group in the first place. 'Rational, selfish, outcome-oriented actors will never choose to co-operate.'[17] Olson writes, in *The logic of collective action*:

> It is often taken for granted, at least where economic objectives are involved, that groups of individuals with common interests usually attempt to further those common interests. Groups of individuals with common interests are expected to act on behalf of their common interests much as single individuals are often expected to act on behalf of their personal interests. ... if the members of some group have a common interest or objective, and if they would all be better off if that objective were achieved, it has been thought to follow logically that the individuals in that group would, if they were rational and self-interested, act to achieve that objective. But ... it does not follow, because all of the individuals in a group would gain if they achieved their group objective, that they would act to achieve that objective, even if they were all rational and self-interested. Indeed, unless the number of individuals in a group is quite small, or unless there is coercion or some other special device to make individuals act in their common interest, rational, self-interested individuals will not act to achieve their common or group interests.[18]

Olson's approach is characterised by Ostrom and Ahn as a 'first generation' study.[19] Later analyses have noted reservations to his analysis by considering a series of additional considerations. For Russell Hardin, morals, politics and personal wishes come in as 'extra-rational'.[20] Ostrom has modelled a range of circumstances in which two further conditions apply. One is that people can communicate about their decisions; that in itself has a major impact on the options they choose. The second is that people are able to apply sanctions, formally or informally, for non-cooperation. In behavioural experiments, these

---

[17] J Elster, 1985, Rationality, morality and collective action, *Ethics* 96 (1) 136–55, pp 139, 146.

[18] M Olson, 1971, *The logic of collective action*, Cambridge, MA: Harvard University Press, pp 1–2.

[19] E Ostrom, T Ahn, 2003, *Foundations of social capital*, Cheltenham: Edward Elgar.

[20] R Hardin, 1982, *Collective action*, London: Routledge, ch 8.

sanctions are pervasive, which may be influenced by the unfamiliar setting where these things are being negotiated; but in theoretical terms, voluntarily negotiated settlements – circumstances where people are able both to communicate and to agree the terms – yield better options than either individual decisions, or sanctions alone.[21]

These critiques start by accepting the validity of the basic analysis; they depend on qualifications and shifts in the parameters, rather than alternative models. But there is an obvious problem with the assertion that people 'will not act to achieve their common or group interests' – it is just not true. We do not have to look very far to find counter-examples. If people never joined groups out of self-interest, there would be no business partnerships, no joint ownership and no shareholders. (In a world consisting of rational, self-interested people who refused to cooperate with anyone else, it is debatable whether there would be any marriages, families, religious congregations or social clubs; but, in fairness, Olson does specify that he is talking about economic groups.) If people did not join large groups, but stuck to small ones, there would be no mutual insurance, no building societies, no public companies and no social institutions. Groups of individuals who share a common interest do indeed collaborate to further those interests.

The analysis of collective action offered in these theories depends on an assumption about the interests of rational individual actors. A very strange construction is being put on 'rationality'. A rational, self-interested person makes a calculation about participation, based on the costs and benefits entailed in the process, and does so consistently. There is nothing intrinsically implausible about that proposition, but it cannot be assumed that all rational actors will be faced with the same choice, or that such a calculation must always deliver the same outcome for everyone, regardless of the costs and benefits. Consider, for example, the situation of a doctor, trained in the United Kingdom and about to embark on a medical career after qualification. The same doctor can commit to working in the UK or go to work in the US for a markedly higher salary. If the doctor is rational, self-interested and outcome oriented, there is a calculation to make. Perhaps the doctor will leave, perhaps not; but the conclusion of that calculation is not foregone. In practice, while the number of doctors who move to the US is substantial, most doctors who do make that decision opt for their

---

[21] E Ostrom, J Walker, R Gardner, 1992, Covenants with and without a sword: self-governance is possible, *American Political Science Review* 86 (2) 404–17.

own good reasons to stay in the UK. Among the costs they face are the loss of community, family and social networks, and the positive costs of integrating into a new, somewhat different culture. We can, if we wish, add other emotive, irrational or extra-rational reasons for staying, but the crucial flaw in the methodology is not that people might not act in a self-interested way; it is that they may well be doing just that, and the theory is framed in a way that prevents us from knowing if that is the case. Modelling people's behaviour through game theory or 'rational choice' does not generally allow for variations in individual preferences, or the elasticity of people's responses – elements that are basic to economic analysis. The analysis falls foul of precisely the same charge that individualist theories commonly levy against collectivism: it supposes that everyone will act the same way.

The many and the few

Individuals and minorities may well have interests that diverge from the interests of the groups they are part of. In formal economic theory, this modest proposition tends to be transmuted into the much more contentious assertion that individual interests must always diverge from the group's; but it is not necessary to make that jump to see that there is a problem. Wherever there are such differences, there is a genuine risk that giving more weight to the interests of collectives will override the interests of individuals or minorities within those groups.

Social science is based on generalisation – it needs to be, because people are rarely unanimous about anything – and generalisations tend to pass over individual eccentricities. While I was pointing to the extraordinarily high levels of consensus of choices, some readers might reasonably have objected that if 97% of households have a washing machine, it follows that 3% do not. Perhaps some people in the 3% would like one; but perhaps there are some people, even if there are not very many, who choose not to have one. There are exceptions to almost all indicators of social behaviour. There are always going to be some people who choose to do things differently – living in boats, sleeping in the open air, going barefoot or whatever. Is it possible, then, for there ever to be a social preference, or some accepted understanding of social welfare? If that question means that preferences must be uniformly and unanimously approved by everyone without exception, the answer is probably 'no'. Some people, after all, enjoy a good war; some people choose invasive medical treatment in preference to good health (Munchausen's Syndrome is a recognised pathology); some people like to be tortured, and will even pay other people to do it to them. Having said that, the challenge can be turned on its head – there is never going to be any uniform or unequivocal view of what constitutes individual welfare, either.[22]

The theoretical literature tends to take it for granted that if there is any difference between the preferences expressed by individuals and the preferences expressed through a collective process, it is the preferences of individuals that must have priority. In Arrow's model, priorities must depend 'only on the orderings of individuals'. (The phrase is smuggled into his consideration of the 'independence of irrelevant alternatives'.) In a quite different argument, but in the same vein, Kaplow and Shavell argue that any collective organisation compromises the distribution that will maximise welfare.[23] Their basis for saying that is that only individual preferences can determine what welfare is, and anything which does not respect those preferences must mean that people are worse off. Both these examples suppose that preferences expressed by individuals are a 'gold standard', the test for everything else. That precludes the possibility of coming to a different conclusion, for example, through democratic deliberation or consistency with legal rules. If there is a conflict between a group decision and the preferences of individuals, it is not obvious that it is the group decision which should be discounted. Once it is accepted that groups may come to legitimate decisions by following their own processes, List and Pettit demonstrate that it is possible to construct a model of group action that justifies participation in groups. This is true even if we accept the assumptions and constraints of the impossibility theorem.[24]

What happens, however, when people's interests really do diverge? Small differences in patterns of behaviour do not matter much for the purposes of description or generalised analysis. They are much more important when it comes to the normative aspects. If the vast majority of people in a society choose or act in one way, can they ever reasonably require individuals to conform? Liberal individualism begins from the strong normative presumption that individuals within a society may reasonably differ. As J S Mill famously argued:

> If all mankind minus one were of one opinion, and only
> one person were of the contrary opinion, mankind would

22 A Sen, 2002, *Rationality and freedom*, Cambridge, MA: Belknap Press, p 27.

23 L Kaplow, S Shavell, 2001, Any non-welfarist method of policy assessment violates the Pareto Principle, *Journal of Political Economy* 109 (2) 281–7.

24 C List, P Pettit, 2011, *Group agency*, Oxford: Oxford University Press; T Isaacs, 2011, *Moral responsibility in collective contexts*, Oxford: Oxford University Press.

be no more justified in silencing that one person than he, if
he had the power, would be justified in silencing mankind.[25]

That principle extends beyond free speech. If there are individual
rights – a right to live differently – those rights exist regardless of
whether the mass of the population wants something else to happen.

Even within the liberal paradigm, there are some circumstances
in which the majority of people can justifiably require the minority
to conform. There are many rules and regulations, some to protect
other people, some to safeguard the individual, some (like the rules
of the road) are there simply to make social life possible. There are
circumstances where some people would argue that the rules recognise
the force of numbers – for example, removing the property rights of
someone whose house stands in the way of a development. That is a
question of balancing one set of rights against others, which is normally
resolved through a group process such as government and arbitration.
I will come back to those processes in due course, but at this point
I want to examine the implications of the opposing argument: that there
are circumstances where the rights of individuals cannot legitimately
be set aside.

In many cases, those rights are constructed as liberties, and the only
obligation is not to interfere with them; but there are also 'claim rights',
where the rights that people hold impose obligations on others.[26]
People who can communicate only in a minority language can call for
interpretation at a court hearing, on the basis that it is not a fair hearing
if people are unable to hear the arguments against themselves. People
with disabilities can look, under UK law, for reasonable adjustments
to be made by public agencies. The Scottish Government has recently
proposed a National Plan for British Sign Language, recognising the
existence of a minority population which does not have the option of
spoken communication in a way that is open to everyone else. The 60-
point plan includes provision to engage school pupils who can hear to
learn the language so they can communicate with those who cannot.[27]

The general principle here is based on an assertion of people's rights.
These are cases where a minority of people make demands on a much

---

[25] J S Mill, 1851, On Liberty, ch 2.
[26] W Hohfeld, 1920, *Some fundamental legal conceptions as applied in judicial reasoning*,
New Haven, CT: Yale University Press, obtained at archive.org.
[27] Scottish Government, 2017, *Scottish Government British Sign Language (BSL) National
Plan 2017–2023*, Edinburgh: Scottish Government, www.gov.scot/Resource/
0052/00526382.pdf, last obtained 28 September 2018.

larger group – in the case of BSL, quite a small minority – and would be disadvantaged if things do not change. It is easy to justify putting obligations on people where they are doing something directly to the detriment of others – for example, polluting the water supply, causing floods, creating risks to public health or the like – but these examples are different. The duties fall on other people because of the position of the rights-holder, not because of the conduct of the person being obliged.

As soon as we accept the possibility that we, or other people, may have to defer to the rights of a minority, we implicitly acknowledge the possibility that in other cases a minority may have to cede to the rights of a majority. If people have to conform to the rights of others, then in some cases larger groups will have to defer to smaller ones; and in others, the opposite may be true. The Universal Declaration of Human Rights represents international acknowledgement of people's right to social security:

> Everyone, as a member of society, has the right to social security and is entitled to realization, through national effort and international co-operation and in accordance with the organization and resources of each State, of the economic, social and cultural rights indispensable for his dignity and the free development of his personality.[28]

That is framed as an individual right, but in developed societies at least, the vast majority of the population will have and exercise such rights at some point of their lives, imposing obligations on others while they do so.

This is not about counting heads; it is about rights and obligations. Resolving the balance of power between individuals, minorities and majorities is not a question of numbers. In the *Federalist Papers*, a series of documents explaining the rationale behind the US constitution, James Madison defined a 'faction' in society as 'a number of citizens, whether amounting to a minority or majority of the whole, who are united and actuated by some common impulse of passion, or of interest, adverse to the rights of other citizens, or to the permanent and aggregate interests of the community'.[29] It cannot be assumed that the rights which have priority are always the rights of individuals in

---

[28] United Nations, 1948, Universal Declaration of Human Rights, Article 22.
[29] J Madison, 1788, *Federalist Papers 10*, New York: Mentor, 1961, p 78.

isolation. The few may have to allow the many, for example, to enforce the rights of third parties, such as children; to take steps to prevent free riding, and to ensure the equitable distribution of burdens and benefits; and, of course, in cases where, as a result of received procedure, a decision is arrived at through a majority vote. The central principle has to be that decisions are reached legitimately through an agreed procedure, in ways which respect the relevant rights of all parties.

Protecting individuals within collective structures

There are good reasons for thinking that people within this web of relationships need some protections. People need a certain amount of personal security and protection against exploitation, regardless of whether that is done by groups, or just by other people. The position of an individual, relative to most groups, is asymmetric; there is an imbalance of power. (This is not an issue that is unique to social groups: the same problems of asymmetry might equally apply when powerless individuals have to deal with powerful ones.) Groups have the potential to override individual preferences, for several reasons: they can do things that individuals alone cannot do, the individual is always outnumbered (by definition), and some of the roles that people are required to follow may put them at a disadvantage.

The basic mechanism needed to protect individuals is a structure of rights – in their simplest form, a set of norms that can be enforced through the action of the people whose interests are being infringed. Rights are attached to the person who is most immediately affected by them. Some of these rights are general, applying to everyone in a similar situation; some are particular, being created by personal agreement or contract. Both general and particular rights might simply be 'moral', which means only that people can base a claim on them, and convey an expectation about how other people will behave in any given situation; but many are legal rights, enforceable in courts. So we have, for example, the rights of workers being protected within their employment or the rights of children within families. Both are, at one and the same time, rights of individuals against other individuals, and rights of individuals against the groups they are part of.

It needs to be recognised, too, that groups do not only affect the position of people who are members of the group; they also have the power to exclude, in which case the conflict of the individual and the group lies between insiders and outsiders. If a group is formed for the mutual advantage of its members, Buchanan suggests, it is likely to have an optimum size – a point at which the marginal cost of taking on new members will exceed the benefits of doing so.[30] Jordan extends this into a general theory of poverty and social exclusion; societies are likely to exclude outsiders who require support.[31] Some forms of exclusion imply simply that people are left out – for example, that they may not be able to take advantage of the facilities that group members have, such as pensions. In other cases, steps may be taken to exclude people more actively. Box 4.1 considers one of the most pressing contemporary examples of that mechanism, the status of migrants. The exclusion of migrants may be expressed and experienced through positive sanctions – including the loss of personal liberty and physical restraint – which are comparable to the punishments inflicted on criminals.

Box 4.1: The status of migrants

The United Nations estimates the number of international migrants in the world as 258 million, and that figure is rising.[32] A little over half of that movement is to Europe or America. The total is made up of people who have moved to different countries; if the definition of a migrant was taken to include people who have moved between regions, it would be more than a billion.[33]

This has posed a dilemma for countries which accept a degree of universalism – the principle that people share common rights and need to be treated consistently. If there are human rights, they apply to everyone; the national character of legal institutions usually means that this is transmuted to read, everyone within that country. But citizenship, in the formal sense, is also 'a tie entailing mutual obligations between categorically defined persons and the state'.[34] If there is an inclusive idea of 'citizenship', in the sense used by Lister,[35] that should in principle extend to people who have come to live in a society – but the very idea of citizenship presumes membership of a community, and the process that defines some people as members also identifies others as non-members.

---

[30] Buchanan, 1965, p 9.

[31] B Jordan, 1996, *A theory of poverty and social exclusion*, Brighton: Polity Press.

[32] UN Population Division, 2017, International migrant stock 2017, www.un.org/en/development/desa/population/migration/data/estimates2/estimates17.shtml, last obtained 28 September 2018.

[33] United Nations Department of Economic and Social Affairs, 2013, *Cross-national comparisons of internal migration*, New York: United Nations.

[34] C Tilly, 1997, A primer on citizenship, *Theory and Society* 26 (4) 599–602.

[35] R Lister, 1990, *The exclusive society*, London: CPAG.

The political and social tensions, Banting and Kymlicka argue, are not generated by the numbers of migrants as such, but rather by the pace of change.[36] Integration takes time. The circumstances of migrant or 'guest' workers, 'economic' migrants (that is, people seeking a better life) and people who come to join families are likely to be ambiguous. When people move from one society to another, they may retain links to their former community: one of the principal sources of income for some developing countries is 'remittances', the money that migrant workers send home. Within their new environments, migrants often rely on fellow migrants to establish networks of contact and support.[37]

There has been a general trend towards multicultural policy – generally intended to indicate acceptance and tolerance of differences, rather than an insistence that people should integrate into the host society[38] – but in recent years many countries have introduced citizenship tests, generally designed to ensure that the migrant will accept certain conditions before admission to full rights in the host society.[39] That implies, of necessity, a range of possible statuses: residents, applicants for citizenship, immigrants and those who have none of those statuses, including illegal residents. There are also classes of migrants for whom, by international convention, the general standards applying to the host population should be extended: stateless persons, asylum seekers and refugees. (The provision in practice is often grudging.) Migrants do not necessarily have the same entitlements as people in the host community, especially in circumstances where entitlements are particular and based in a record of contribution. There is a risk that even if their citizenship is recognised, in the absence of particular rights they will be second-class citizens at best.

The individual and the collective: moral perspectives

There are certainly situations where individuals are confined and oppressed by groups. However, the moral objections to collectivism suffer, like the criticisms made from methodological individualism, from a tendency to overstate its evils. All sorts of bad things – the

---

[36] K Banting, W Kymlicka, 2006, Immigration, multiculturalism, and the welfare state, *Ethics and International Affairs*, 20 (3) 281–304, pp 292–3.

[37] P Craven, B Wellman, 1973, The network city, *Sociological Inquiry* 43 (3–4) 57–88, p 58.

[38] Banting, Kymlicka, 2006, p 288.

[39] S Goodman, 2014, *Immigration and membership politics in Western Europe*, Cambridge: Cambridge University Press.

repression of sexuality, racism, control of people's bodies or restrictions on the position of women – are attributed to collectives. But many of these problems are not intrinsically the problems of collectivism at all. They are more to do with morality, and while it is true that some collective codes reinforce repressive morality, people who make repressive moral judgments are liable to make them in one-to-one, interpersonal relationships, not just in groups.

In relation to control of people's bodies, it is also important to recognise that some of the individual choices that people might otherwise make are restricted by the nature of their individual rights, not just by collective action. It would be self-contradictory to accept, in the name of liberty, that people can do things which take all their liberty away, so we do not accept that people can sell themselves into slavery, or be enslaved by drugs, or that they can sign away all their future rights. We do not accept that people can sell their vital organs, or agree to be eaten.[40] Despite the protests which met the Spanner trial, there are degrees of physical harm, such as torture and mutilation, that no one can or should be able to consent to.[41] (I promised no invented examples; this is not a thought experiment.)

There are certainly cases where the conduct of individuals is constrained by public morality. Box 4.2 looks at crime and punishment – circumstances in which individuals may legitimately be restricted, controlled or harmed by society as a group. Upholding the criminal law might be abused, but it is not necessarily a bad thing to do, and it points to a general principle. Regardless of the liberal advocacy of tolerance, most people are inclined to believe that the morals that they accept as right and wrong – for example, not to kill, to steal or to do violence to others – apply to others as well as to themselves. If the basis of morals is consequentialist, principled or virtue-based – anything other than particularist – it would be inconsistent to think differently. There are moral codes that make a point of not being judgmental, but the point of morality is to help us evaluate conduct: if certain conduct is better, other conduct is worse.

---

[40] L Harding, 2003, Victim of cannibal agreed to be eaten, *The Guardian*, 4 December, https://www.theguardian.com/world/2003/dec/04/germany.lukeharding, last obtained 28 September 2018.

[41] V Bergelson, 2008, Autonomy, dignity and consent to harm, *Rutgers Law Review*, 60 (3) 723–36.

Box 4.2: Crime and punishment

There are no private crimes; criminal activity is always a public matter. That is true by definition. The criminal law declares what is, and what is not, a matter for public concern. Domestic violence used to be seen as a private matter, and was not criminal; but the law has been changing in many jurisdictions, so that it is considered to fall in the public sphere.[42] Some actions are criminal, not because they are obviously immoral, but because the law says so; a publican can be convicted of a criminal offence because a member of staff has served alcohol to someone under age, even if the publican did not know about it or had instructed staff to uphold the law. On the other hand, bullying at school or work, though often intensely unpleasant and distressing, is not usually against the law. Regardless of its immorality or its severity, immoral behaviour becomes criminal only when it is forbidden by law.

There are at least five main arguments for punishing crimes.[43] The first is retribution: returning evil for evil. That principle is not universally accepted – the Christian position, or at least the position in the Sermon of the Mount, is one of returning good for evil – but it is very widely held. There are supplementary arguments about the supposed benefit of retribution. In game theory, 'tit for tat' emerges as a robust and sustainable policy,[44] but fundamentally it rests on the principle of reciprocity; that, for many people, is justice.

The second purpose of punishment is to convey public disapproval. The strength of the punishment reflects, not just the harm that is done, but the abhorrence that people feel for the crime; sexual crimes are punished rather more severely than malicious wounding. However, people's reaction to different crimes changes over time – for example, bigamy is no longer treated as a serious threat to others – and the severity of the punishment tends to shift with those perceptions.

Third, there is correction. Punishment is seen as a form of education, which guides people to the correct path. Related to that there is rehabilitation: reforming and reintegrating the offender.

---

[42] M Fineman, R Mykitiuk, 1994, *The public nature of private violence*, New York: Routledge.

[43] P Bean, 1981, *Punishment*, Oxford: Martin Robertson.

[44] G Axelrod, 1990, *The evolution of co-operation*, Harmondsworth: Penguin.

Fourth, there is containment. People who are in prison are not supposed to be able to commit further crimes while they are there (or if they do, they are presumed to commit them on other prisoners rather than the general public).

Fifth, there is deterrence: the belief that punishment will lead other people not to do the same thing. There is little or no evidence to support this belief – stealing sheep became less prevalent after people were no longer being hanged for it – but it is widely believed.

Correction and rehabilitation might be justified in terms of individualism. They become particularly important in the treatment of young offenders, because justice in those cases is tempered by a concern for child welfare. But individualist responses play only a limited role – for example, compensation for criminal acts or restorative justice, where criminals are expected to take account of the views of their victims, are still only a marginal part of judicial systems in the West.

The other arguments for punishment are different. The principal focus of retribution, deterrence, containment or public disapproval is not the offender, but the society of which they are part. They will be pursued even if the consequences for the offender are bad. They are meant to be bad for the offender – that is the point. Punishment is done for society, not the individual who is punished. The moral justification for punishment is collective.

There is some justice in another criticism of collectivism: that the emphasis on the group has a tendency to override the individual characteristics of the people within it. Collectivism is built around a view of people's relationships with other people, not a study of the whole person: people in groups are defined by their roles.[45] Participation in social groups depends on people adopting roles – parent, employee, representative, pupil, supporter and so on. Even if the roles are complex, overlapping and personal, the picture can never be quite complete. That does not mean, however, that collectivism must lead to the sort of repression or conformity that is assumed by its libertarian critics. Collective action is a way to increase people's capacity, to empower them, to make it possible for them to achieve their ends. It is legitimate when it increases people's autonomy, capacity, power and choice; it ceases to be legitimate when it restricts them. There is a distinction between the rule of law and repression, between education and indoctrination,

---

[45] R Dahrendorf, 1973, *Homo sociologicus*, London: Routledge and Kegan Paul.

between cooperation and forced labour; it is always necessary to make judgments about how far any action should go.

It is probably fair to object, too, that collectivism asserts the rights and duties of a group, a society or a nation, to the disadvantage of the rights and duties of the individual. 'Communities work', Bowles and Gintis argue, 'because they are good at enforcing norms, and whether this is a good thing depends on what the norms are.'[46] It is perfectly true that the rights and conduct of groups might conflict with the rights and conduct of individuals, but that is not necessarily because they are groups. There are, after all, examples where the rights of some individuals are used against the rights of others – property rights are an obvious example, where some people have the right to exclude others from access to the essentials of daily life. Corporate bodies, as well as individuals, can own and control property. There may well be an issue when collective groups – churches, employers and governments – adopt positions which are contrary to minority or individual interests – but that is not because they are groups, and nor is it because groups are intrinsically repressive in themselves; it is because groups have the capacity to do lots of things, good and bad, and there are moral choices to be made.

It might reasonably be said that the conflict of individual and collective rights is exaggerated, but there is a genuine tension between collectivism and individualism nevertheless. Social groups are composed of people; people are individual in some respects and occupy roles in others. Sometimes the roles that people are asked to fill are so all-encompassing that little or no space is left for the individual. That may happen, for example, in traditional families, where the restrictions on women in particular are so extensive that they are left no options for individual expression. It can happen in some types of employment, where people's waking hours are wholly taken up with the demands of their role as employees. It can happen in some forms of military service – that is increasingly rare in modern, professional armies, but there are still countries where it is true. And it can happen in some forms of religious practice, and indeed in totalitarian societies, where – as the name suggests – everything about a person's behaviour is prescribed for them. But it would be absurd to conclude that a free society should have no family, no military, no employment and no religion. The relationships that make us part of collective groups are part of our lives.

---

[46] S Bowles, H Gintis, 2002, Social capital and community governance, *Economic Journal* 112 F419–F436.

5

Community

The nature of a community

'Community' may seem to be a fairly vague idea. In a well-known article, Hillery identified 94 different definitions of the term. 'All the definitions deal with people. Beyond this common basis, there is no agreement.'[1] Much of the scepticism about the idea of community has arisen because early ideas about it were tied to an idealised model, based on social relations in a local neighbourhood. Many of the definitions of community considered and rejected by Stacey in the 1960s were territorial; she argued for a focus on a 'local social system' instead.[2] Some communities are local, but many are not; to understand what community really means, it helps to move away from a territorial model altogether.

A community, like a society, is a set of networks. The idea of a society refers to a range of interconnected, overlapping networks, institutions and social groups; the term generally refers to the full range of those networks. A 'community' is also a set of networks, but the term is used across the full range of such systems, from the smallest to the largest. Communities range from microcosms of society – for example, the identification of a community with a school or a neighbourhood – all the way to national and international networks. The term could refer to the networks of a local area, to a segment of the population (such as the 'Muslim community' or the 'business community'), possibly to the whole society itself, perhaps extending to relationships across social boundaries (such as the Jewish diaspora or the scientific community). There are communities that are based on location – neighbourhoods, towns, regions – but others are based on other types of connection between people, such as tribal identity, religion, common activities, patterns of interaction or mutual responsibility. There can be a community of students, or nurses, or activists, or former members

[1] G Hillery, 1955, Definitions of community: areas of agreement, *Rural Sociology* 20 111–23.
[2] M Stacey, 1969, The myth of community studies, *British Journal of Sociolog*, 20 (2) 134–47.

of the armed forces. People can belong to many communities at the same time.

A 'community' is not necessarily a description of the full range of social relationships, but nor is it an organisation or group in itself. From the point of view of a single person, a community is experienced through a range of linkages and networks with other people and groups. 'Network analysis', Craven and Wellman explain, works by tracking the personal linkages of people within complex settings.

> This approach emphasizes such questions as 'Who is linked to whom?', 'What is the content of their relationship?', and 'What is the structure of their relational network?' ... There will be networks characterized by both a high density of ties between members and a relative paucity of ties outside a defined network boundary. From a network perspective, these bounded sets of links and nodes, all of whose members are connected either directly or via indirect paths of short length, are communities.[3]

It may help to think of these links as a spider's web, sometimes patchy, sometimes thin, and getting thinner as the connections grow more distant. Then superimpose a picture of another person's connections on the first, then another, and another, and so on. The web gets overlain with other webs; the lines get thicker; the picture gets messier and more opaque. As more people are considered, there will be clusters, blobs and patterns, and it makes less and less sense to try to track the patterns individually. This tangle of lines is a way of representing a community. Using a similar metaphor, we refer to some communities as 'tight-knit', while others are 'loosely knit'. The central lesson to draw from both metaphors is that there is not one connection, but many.

Hillery complained that there was no empirical evidence to suggest that all the people in a community shared any of the features identified with community – interaction, common sentiment, norms, institutions, activities or space – with everyone else.[4] That is probably true, but there is no call for them to do so. The boundaries of a community are typically fuzzy, because at the margins some people will be less well integrated than others. The networks that people are part of stretch from the most immediate, in ever wider circles, at least to the level of

---

[3] P Craven, B Wellman, 1973, The network city, *Sociological Inquiry* 43 (3–4) 57–88.
[4] G Hillery, 1959, A critique of selected community concepts, *Social Forces* 37 (3) 237–42.

a society. Like a society, the networks of a community are complex, because for everyone within a community there will be different relationships – families, neighbours, friends, schoolmates and so on; some people may be more firmly integrated into the community, some less so. The more those relationships reinforce each other, the stronger the community will be. Community work, outlined in Box 5.1, is an attempt to build on and strengthen such networks.

Box 5.1: Community work

There are many varieties of community work. Community development has been concerned to improve the capacities and skills in a community or neighbourhood, to build 'social capital' – the resources that come from people supporting each other through expertise, skills, information and common resources.[5] Typically, perhaps paradoxically, that is done in places where there is little sense of community, because that is where the need is greatest. Some forms of community development are done by promoting schemes that change the dynamics and networks in a community, and promote social cohesion – the process by which people accept mutual social responsibilities. Community education, exemplified in the work of Paulo Freire,[6] builds the capacity, skills, networks and power of people in disadvantaged circumstances. Community action, also known as community organisation, aims to help people in poorer areas to get a sense of community, and to help poorer communities exercise power through collective action. This is the form of collective action mainly advocated by Saul Alinsky, an inspiration for both Barack Obama (who had worked as a community organiser) and Hillary Clinton (who wrote a thesis about Alinsky). Alinsky saw community action as a galvanising force that could both help to redress the imbalance of power and equip communities with the capacities and skills they needed.[7]

This kind of work can be difficult. The core problem rests, not in the methods (which are used effectively in areas such as the welfare of older people or health promotion), but in the disadvantage and social isolation of the communities that the workers are trying to help. Describing an area as 'poor' says more than the statement that poor people live there. The most deprived areas are marked not just by the low relative income and resources of residents, but by social isolation,

[5] P Henderson, D Thomas, 2013, *Skills in neighbourhood work*, London: Routledge, ch 1.
[6] P Freire, 1972, *The pedagogy of the oppressed*, Harmondsworth: Penguin.
[7] S Alinsky, 1989, *Rules for radicals*, New York: Random House.

transient populations, limited facilities and weak community organisation. What distinguishes them from other, more successful communities is both a higher incidence of social problems, and the relative absence or weakness of relationships, structures and capacities which are available elsewhere. The main resource that community workers have to draw on is likely to be the capacities and engagement of the people who are in the communities, and the reason why those capacities are not engaged at the outset is that those people lack the resources to make a difference. Developing social capital or empowering communities are typically treated as 'bootstrap' operations – expecting people in the poorest and most deprived circumstances to pull themselves up by their own efforts. However, as Martin Luther King once commented, it's a cruel jest to say that people should pull themselves up by their bootstraps when they have no boots.[8]

Despite the limitations, there are three good arguments for focusing on deprived communities and neighbourhoods. The first is that areas matter. Some areas have serious problems – security, ill health, environmental problems, lack of facilities. They can be difficult and damaging for the people who live there – not just for poorer people, but for everyone. The second is that wherever people are disadvantaged, they need the kinds of support, facilities and opportunities that will help to make their lives better. A great deal can be done at the local level – providing amenities, activities, opportunities, creating jobs, increasing income and helping to care. The third is that people need a voice. Voice is not the only thing that is needed to empower a population – rights, accountability and community organisation matter – but the less people are heard, the more important it is that they should be.

Because 'community' is such a broad category, the range of activities that might be included under it are manifold; almost any sort of social network might, at times, be described as a community. For Bob Pinker, the idea of a community is linked to personal, informal, affective and traditional ties – a constellation of ideas similar to Tonnies' conception of *Gemeinschaft*. That view of community may be attractive, but it is too diffuse and informal to offer much guidance in the organisation and delivery of services:

It seems that when our policy makers reach an intellectual impasse they cover their embarrassment with the fig leaf

---

[8]   M L King, 1967, Interview on NBC News, https://www.youtube.com/watch?v=2xsbt3a7K-8, last obtained 28 September 2018.

of community. It happened in the case of the Seebohm Committee, when it failed to discover a specific definition of 'the family' and immediately proceeded to extol the virtues of 'the community', which ... came to mean everybody and everything. ... the concept of community can never be sufficiently well defined to serve as a framework for formal and equitable social policies.[9]

It is certainly difficult to reconcile the messy patchwork associated with community with the kind of universalist or rights-based approach that has been dominant in the literature of social policy. The networks that people depend on are different for different people, which is not a promising start for the delivery of services on a stable, consistent basis. But there are different ways of looking at the issues, and a range of concepts of community have been used as vehicles for policy.

Patterns of community

Sharing characteristics, common activities, common values or beliefs is not enough to make a community. That statement might initially seem implausible – it is easier to see its truth when we move from abstract generalities to more concrete examples. People are not said to be members of a 'community' because they all have short sight (a common characteristic), watch nature programmes on television (a common activity), think that children should be disciplined by physical force (a shared value) or believe they have been abducted by aliens (a shared belief). The networks of a community depend on a different kind of social relation. Within any community, there has to be some pattern of interaction, and a relationship between the participants. In other words, a community has to be a social group.

Some of the uses of 'community' are obscure, but a few patterns of community are frequently referred to. One relates to cultural identity: people in minority ethnic groups, people who speak minority languages and groups with a common history may band together. There are various ways of referring to cultural groupings – ethnicity, religious affiliation, language and tribal affiliation among them. This is sometimes referred to simply as a community of 'identity', but all communities

---

[9] R Pinker, 1982, Report of the Working Party on the Role and Tasks of Social Workers: an alternative view, in J Offer, R Pinker (eds) 2017, *Social policy and welfare pluralism*, Bristol: Policy Press, p 128.

share identity to a degree; it is the emphasis on culture, shared activities and the mutual interaction that follows that distinguishes the character of the community.

A second form of community is a community of interest: people engaged in similar kinds of activities, such as business, leisure, religion or patterns of work, may well be brought into contact with each other, engage in mutual support or identify themselves in those terms. If there can be said to be a 'disabled community', it is primarily a community of interest: it may not be true that an older blind person will identify directly, or have a relationship with, someone with learning disabilities, but people with shared issues (such as people with multiple sclerosis, mental illness, hearing loss or visual impairments) often make arrangements to support each other, and then those groups link with other groups to discuss areas like benefits and local services, where they have common concerns.

A third form is community of place: people who live in the same geographical area – a neighbourhood, or town, or region – come into contact with each other, share certain facilities, and are affected by a common physical, social and economic environment. The attempt to build communities in these terms was basic to the development of urban planning, in the form of model communities and urban design; the process is outlined in Box 5.2.

Box 5.2: Urban planning

The idea of community has sometimes been approached as if it referred to a whole, integrated society in microcosm. Urban planning was conceived as a way of developing communities harmoniously with the people who lived in them. Octavia Hill, one of the founders of housing management, wrote: 'You cannot deal with the people and their houses separately. The principle on which the whole work rests, is that the inhabitants and their surroundings must be improved together.'[10] Housing, physical design, the environment and the layout of cities were inseparable from social relationships and the experience of community. The model communities of the Industrial Revolution – Robert Owen's New Lanark and New Harmony, Fourier's Phalanstère, and Howard's 'garden cities' (see Figure 5.1) – were intended not just to improve the environment, but to change the lives of the people who lived in them. In the period when the 'welfare state' was being founded in the UK, new towns were planned that would offer people a different kind of life.

---

[10] O Hill, 1875, *Homes of the London poor*, London: Frank Cass, 51.

Figure 5.1: Ebenezer Howard's 'Three Magnets' 1898[11]

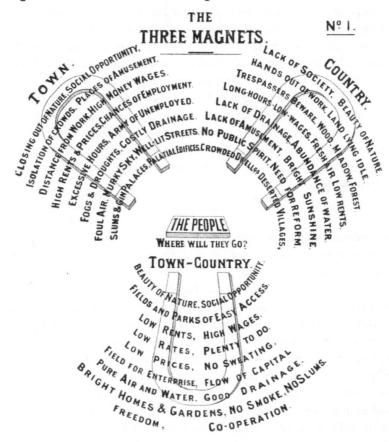

The central problem with this kind of holistic social model is not that such communities cannot be constructed, but that they do not exist in isolation from a broader society; a community is a system of networks, and society is another system of networks that overlaps substantially with it. Often, communities are defined in terms of economic and social phenomena, such as location, shared economic interests or industrial organisation. It has been argued that some communities are 'contrived' instrumentally as a means to lever resources for deprived groups.[12] In the context of a society undergoing economic and social

---

[11] E Howard, 1902, *Garden cities of tomorrow*, London: Swan Sonnenschein, obtained at http://www.gutenberg.org/ebooks/46134

[12] M Shaw, 2008, Community development and the politics of community, in G Craig, M Mayo, K Popple, M Shaw, M Taylor (eds) *The community development reader*, Bristol: Policy Press, pp 305–6.

change, the planner increasingly came to be seen as someone who allocated or negotiated access to resources, such as land use, rather than being an urban designer.[13] In the 1970s, planners were being encouraged to exploit 'planning gains' – to get developers to offer community services or other sorts of community benefit in return for permission to build. As the political balance has switched towards market economics, however, the ambition of using this kind of planning to build a better society has faded. If markets determine the allocation of resources, planners do not. Planners have been recast as custodians of the environment rather than people who shape patterns of housing, transport and communication. They are increasingly seen as adjudicators in disputes – and are expected to apply quasi-judicial criteria in their judgments, including neutrality and consistency.

It is perhaps important here to re-emphasise that the neighbourhood local areas relate only to one sense of community, and it may not be the most important sense. Much of the literature concerned with 'community studies' in the past was highly localised, and if the critiques which emerged could not find a coherent sense of community, it was usually because the evidence was focused on location instead. It used to be true as a general proposition that people would live in one place and that their families, social contact, education, commercial, work, religious and leisure activities would all be centred on that same place. I was born into an urban community where my parents, aunts, uncles and grandparents all lived in the same street, and their work was a short walking distance away. That pattern is increasingly unusual; the communities where it is still true are often the least integrated into contemporary society. In developing countries, traditional communities such as those in rural settlements tend to be isolated and disadvantaged; the movement of people to the cities (and possibly to other countries), along with the process of adapting agriculture to the formal economy, has led to a deracination of people from the cultures that previously were dominant. In developed countries, the effects of modern communications, changing working patterns and deindustrialisation have greatly diminished the traditional association of community and place.[14] It has been argued that community of place has not been lost altogether in this process; it is simply different from

---

[13] D Eversley, 1973, *The planner in society*, London: Faber and Faber.
[14] See M Bulmer, 1986, *Neighbours: The work of Philip Abrams*, Cambridge: Cambridge University Press.

the way it used to be. In the context of complex, urban societies, the networks of community and social contact are more likely to be segmented or specialised, coexisting with other networks in a more broadly defined geographical area.[15] Oliver illustrates this in a study of an urban 'black' community: the people in the study were linked to others through association and by giving each other both emotional and material support.[16]

These different types of community have some of the characteristics of social groups. In the first place, people interact with and have relationships to others in a community – that is almost a tautology, because a community is defined by those relationships. Second, though it is less certain to be true, people can usually identify themselves as members of a community; they know it from their location, their culture or their social contacts. They have mental maps of an 'invisible landscape'.[17] People join voluntary groups, a Welsh study suggests, either because they have a strong sense of belonging and want to express it, or because they want to belong.[18] None of those things makes it certain that a community will form, but they are important for community to develop. People who come into contact with each other – for example, through schools, meeting places or places of worship – are liable gradually to develop shared understandings, commitments and mutual responsibilities.

Even if a community is identifiable, even if some community members are engaged, it is the third element of group membership that may be lacking: the capacity for common action. There are examples of common action being taken informally and spontaneously in communities – organising a street party, a garden fete or a demonstration – but they are not frequent events. It can be difficult for a whole community to act collectively; the roles are less clear, the interests often more divergent, the structures that make action possible less well defined. For common action to develop, it helps if there is some kind of organisation, so that people are able to recognise their roles and responsibilities; and so it happens that, in practice, communities gain the capacity to behave as a social group mainly by going through a more

---

[15] K White, A Guest, 2003, Community lost or transformed? Urbanization and social ties, *City and Community* 2 (3) 239–59.

[16] M Oliver, 1988, The urban black community as network, *Sociological Quarterly* 29 (4) 623–45.

[17] C Mercer, 1975, *Living in cities*, Harmondsworth: Penguin, ch 7.

[18] D Dallimore, H Davis, M Eichsteller, R Mann, 2018, Place, belonging and the determinants of volunteering, *Voluntary Sector Review* 9 (1) 21–38.

formal process, appointing representative or participatory groups, either formally or ad hoc, to act in their name. It can be done, for example, by arranging a meeting, forming a club or setting up a committee. The lack of this kind of community organisation has been identified as a significant element in the experience of poverty.[19]

Solidarity in communities

The principle of 'communitarianism' brings together the descriptive elements of community and their moral foundation. In its descriptive sense, communitarianism begins from the same premises as substantive collectivism: that people are born into families, communities and societies; that they have ties and obligations from the outset; and that our nature as people is built up from this kind of relationship. In its moral sense, communitarianism argues that our morals are necessarily personal, particular, dependent on the social context and – of course – communal.

At times, discussions of morals boil down to a question of approving or disapproving of what other people do. That is not the central issue here. The moral obligations which are being discussed are the bonds of solidarity – the sense of mutual responsibility that leads to people in a community doing things with others, and doing things for others. Solidarity is pervasive; it binds us to family, to neighbours and to a broader society. It is in the nature of solidarity that our obligations multiply and grow thicker in relation to the people we are closest to – solidarity is a major part of what makes them close. The closest of these networks is usually a family, but the range of solidaristic networks, both formal and informal, is wide: it can be expressed through organisations, community, regional and national identity. Alfandari writes:

> Solidarity supposes the interdependence of individuals within a defined group. One can imagine a system of concentric circles of solidarity, wider and wider, which go from the nuclear family up to the international community.[20]

The link between solidarity and interdependence is based on our socialisation into a range of obligations, and particularly the principle of reciprocity – the idea that when we have received a good, we have

---

[19] D Narayan, R Chambers, M Shah, P Petesch, 2000, *Voices of the poor: Crying out for change*, New York: World Bank/Oxford University Press, ch 10.

[20] E Alfandari, 1989, *Action et aide sociales*, Paris: Dalloz, p 73.

an obligation to do likewise. With social distance, reciprocity is based on direct exchange; with people who are closer (most obviously, the family), there is generalised reciprocity (circles of exchange that are never quite complete, and do not need to be). Titmuss's 'gift relationship' was based in the argument that this generalised sense, a broad sense that people would do the same for each other, could be harnessed for a whole society.[21] That is uncertain, but there are formal arrangements – such as the provision of pensions – which work on a similar principle: workers now pay for pensioners now, in the expectation that when the time comes, the next generation will pay for them.

This perspective is powerful, but there are several problems with it. First, it can be limiting. Man is born free, Rousseau wrote, but he is everywhere in chains[22]: the effect of subjecting people to obligations from their birth may be to limit what is possible in their lives. The position of women, as an obvious example, is liable to be constrained by structures of familial and caring obligations. Second, solidarity can be exclusive. It defines the people whom each person owes obligations; it identifies, and legitimates, the sense that there is less responsibility to people who are more distant; and, by the same process, it implicitly identifies outsiders and the people to whom there is no responsibility. Third, it can be profoundly unequal – a justification for looking after one's own, but not others. Communitarian values stand in contrast to universalist ones, which hold that the same rules apply to everyone: the most obvious example of universal values might be universal human rights, though some religious codes are also presented as rules for everyone to live by. One of the strongest arguments for universal rules is an argument for consistency: that in the same circumstances, with other things being equal, people should be subject to the same expectations. The communitarian response to that is, of course, that people never really are in the same circumstances, and other things are never equal.

The model of solidarity squares with many people's moral perceptions. Although lots of what is written about morality is couched in universal terms, the truth is that the model does reflect what most people really think – that they have stronger responsibilities for those who are closest to them than they do to others. That is what being close means. Part of the test of the morality of collective action is that such action is consistent with the nature of the groups that take it. For societies to hold together, the relationships that bind them – the ties

---

[21] R Titmuss, 1971, *The gift relationship*, London: Allen and Unwin; and see D Reisman, 1977, *Richard Titmuss: Welfare and society*, London: Heinemann.

[22] J J Rousseau, 1762, *Du contrat social*, I.1.

of solidarity – are fundamental; without those ties, there can be no society. At the same time, communitarian thinking has the potential to be so exclusive as to become immoral. There does not have to be only one way of resolving moral issues. Several writers have argued for 'moderate' particularism, leavened with a range of universal principles and guarantees of the position of individuals within the structure. Amitai Etzioni is a strong advocate of a communitarian social order, but he is also concerned to defend the freedom of the individual.[23] Peter Jones argues that 'strictly, there is no reason why moderate particularism should not also accommodate an idea of universal rights of citizenship – if by that we mean only that there are certain rights which every political community must accord to its members.'[24]

Social inclusion

'By and large', Boulding once wrote, 'it is an objective of social policy to build the identity of a person around some community with which he is associated.'[25] The principle of solidarity implies that in society there will be a range of networks and social groups where people accept responsibility for each other. Some people, however, are not fully part of those networks. They may be 'marginal', connected to solidarity only tenuously; they may be excluded. Exclusion can happen because people are left out of social arrangements, but it can also happen deliberately, because they are shut out (like migrants) or socially rejected – the condition, for example, of people with AIDS. It is not enough to assume that, just because a community exists, people will be part of it; there has to be some kind of process to bring that about. If people are excluded, there need to be steps taken to include them, to make them part of society by bringing them into solidaristic social networks. This process was initially described in France in terms of 'insertion', a term which does not travel well; the language of 'social inclusion' has been taken to refer to the same process.

The initial strategy for social inclusion in France was the movement towards 'generalisation', an attempt progressively to extend the scope of supportive schemes such as social insurance. There are limits to how far that can be done, because insurance depends on people being able

---

[23] A Etzioni, 2004, *From empire to community*, New York: Palgrave Macmillan, pp 24–5.

[24] P Jones, 1990, Universal principles and particular claims, in R Goodin, A Ware (eds) *Needs and welfare*, London: Sage, p 40.

[25] K Boulding, 1973, The boundaries of social policy, in W D Birrell, P Hillyard, A Murie, D Roche (eds) *Social administration*, Harmondsworth: Penguin, p 192.

to make contributions. The *régime général*, a scheme that was supposed to complete coverage for workers who were not part of existing occupational schemes, had reached its limits by the early 1970s. René Lenoir's book *Les Exclus* identified one in ten people in the population who had not been reached by social insurance.[26] Part of the issue was addressed by extending solidarity (for example, the *Allocation de solidarité spécifique*, for long-term unemployed people); the idea of insertion came to refer to the development of new kinds of scheme, aimed at people who were left out. The *Revenu minimum d'insertion* (RMI) was introduced in 1988. The model of the RMI, later renamed the *Revenu de solidarité active* to emphasise the link with work, was hugely influential, spawning imitations in several European countries. It had two main elements. One was the introduction of a basic means-tested benefit, of a type familiar in many other countries. The second element, concerned with insertion, consisted of an agreement made between the service user and the state. Contracts were made between service users and social workers, acting on behalf of the local commission for insertion (CLI). Many contracts consisted simply of an agreement to look for work, and others offered job placements, but others were made to change the circumstances of the excluded person – contracts for employment training, health improvement, household management, literacy courses, conduct or whatever was appropriate for the individual. The reactions of service users were mixed. Many saw the contracts as an imposition, a form of 'workfare'; others saw them as a privilege and demanded them as a right.

> The notion of insertion ... is very badly understood by the beneficiaries. The idea of insertion itself, however understood, is only in the minds of a minority of people who sign contracts. The others put the search for work first as the main objective: 'Anyway, I don't want insertion, I can find work.'[27]

The ideas of solidarity and exclusion have been central to social policy in France, where they served in place of principles such as welfare, rights and poverty that have been dominant in English-speaking countries. When the UK government objected to references to poverty in documents issued by the European Union, the EU shifted

---

[26] R Lenoir, 1974, *Les exclus*, Paris: Seuil.
[27] P Estèbe, N Haydadi, H Sibille, 1991, Le RMI: une raison sociale à la pauvreté?, in *Le RMI à l'épreuve des faits* (Collective work), Paris: Syros, p 61.

its discourse to refer to exclusion instead;[28] from there, the idea has spread to other international organisations, so that the UN has adopted the same discourse. For the UN, 'social exclusion describes a state in which individuals are unable to participate fully in economic, social, political and cultural life, as well as the process leading to and sustaining such a state.'[29]

The implications of this conceptual framework – the concepts of solidarity, inclusion and exclusion – run counter to Pinker's argument that a focus on community cannot offer a sensible focus for policy. But the project of social inclusion – extending solidarity to those who are marginal and excluded – is a process that is always incomplete, not a comprehensive answer to the problems. A focus on communities contributes to the mix of welfare policies, but it can be difficult to reconcile with the emphasis on universalism, rights and social justice that dominates much of the discourse in social policy.

The political community

For Béland and Lecours, the key question for social policy is where the limits of solidarity are set. 'Who should be included in the "social justice" community, or put another way, to whom should social solidarity extend?'[30] The answer to this question lies in the 'political community'. A political community is a set of networks and relationships, defining the institutions and processes through which a society is governed.

The communities that have been discussed up to this point are mainly smaller communities – networks where people have defined relationships, are closer to others in the network, where they recognise the obligations of solidarity. It is possible to see the networks of a society as the product of solidarity in a series of smaller constituent communities. A French government report suggests:

> national solidarity involves at one and the same time the redistribution of available resources, changes which have to be made in social protection, and continuing vigilance

---

[28] Economic and Social Committee, 1993, Opinion on social exclusion, *Official Journal of the European Communities* 93/C 352/13.

[29] UN DESA, 2016, *Leaving no one behind*, New York: United Nations, ST/ESA/362, p 18.

[30] D Béland, A Lecours, 2008, *Nationalism and social policy*, Oxford: Oxford University Press, ch 1.

to ensure that certain social categories are not left out. Because of this, government has to give its support to local forms of solidarity.[31]

The last part of that implies that local solidarities are contributing to a broader national solidarity. It may be the case, however, that the more general forms of solidarity – solidarity at the level of the whole society, or possibly of the nation – are more in evidence, and more meaningful, than solidarities at more local levels. Some broadly defined networks, including groups based on regional identity, ethnicity, language or traditional cultures, may not be associated with any clear collective structure. By contrast, the links between members of the wider society or the political community – groupings which may well seem to be more remote from everyday experience – are potentially strong. People in Carlisle accept a responsibility for people in Cornwall; people in Carcassonne accept a responsibility for people in Cambrai. That is not just down to emotion; it is how things are done.

Most political communities are based around a territory, a citizenry and the state – a system of government. The dominant model is arguably the 'nation state', though in practice many political communities are multinational. Nations are sometimes described, half-dismissively, as 'imagined' communities. Anderson calls the nation state 'imagined' because 'the members of even the smallest nation will never know most of their fellow-members, meet them, or even hear of them, yet in the minds of each lives the image of their communion'.[32] That comment only really makes sense if we expect a community to bring the members into direct contact with each other; as I explained at the beginning of this chapter, that is not how communities work. Communities are based on networks; they consist of interlaced connections between people, and do not have to depend on any high degree of uniformity, commonality or 'communion'.

The literature on nationalism largely focuses on the ways in which nationalist movements forge a national identity. Habermas suggests that:

> Only a national consciousness, crystallized around the notion of a common ancestry, language, and history, only the consciousness of belonging to 'the same' people, makes

---

[31] Cited J-M Belorgey, 1988, *La gauche et les pauvres*, Paris: Syros/Alternatives, p 86.

[32] B Anderson, 2006, *Imagined communities*, London: Verso, p 6.

subjects into citizens of a single political community – into
members who can feel responsible for one another.[33]

The idea of the nation, and national identity, becomes the framework
within which national social policies are developed. However, as
Erika Harris observes, the process of developing a national identity –
emphasising culture, history, and attempting to bind the political
community into a common narrative – is a different process from the
task of building a state and its institutions.[34] Any political community
depends on a complex network of relationships, typically covering
territory, people, government, the structure of laws and relationships
with other such communities. If the political community defines the
patterns of solidarity, it is no less true that the development of solidarity
is critically important for the maintenance of the political community
itself. Political communities – especially those which have a range
of nationalities or ethnicities – have been able to build solidarity in
different ways. Geographical location or territory is obviously a major
element in the definition of most political communities. Gdansk and
Wroclaw used to be in Germany, and are now in Poland; Lviv was
in Poland, and is now in Ukraine. Belgium or Switzerland have not
been held together so much by a unified consciousness, as by practical
arrangements made to accommodate the needs of people in the same
area sharing a society and a polity. And that points to one of the other
elements in the identification of communities, which is commonality
of interests. People who live in the same places share common burdens,
use communal services and facilities, are jointly and severally affected
by the things that affect their country.

The patterns of community discussed in this chapter have included
shared identity and culture, common interests or a distinct geographical
location. Contemporary nation states have all three. However, political
communities, including the nation states, also have something more,
which other communities may not have: a capacity for collective
action. States have a government and a structure of law, and typically
they will have national services and provisions (including, for example,
communications, pensions and health care). They recognise and specify
the rights of citizens, and they determine the framework within which
those rights are realised.

---

[33] J Habermas, 2006, The European nation-state, *Ratio Juris* 9 (2) 125–37.
[34] E Harris, 2009, *Nationalism: Theories and cases*, Edinburgh: Edinburgh University
Press, pp 39–40.

We tend to think of nations or countries as the principal structure within with social policies are conceived and developed. Harris writes:

> As long as the nation state is the main framework – and it is hard to think about political community outside its frame – for solidarity, sovereignty and the exercise of political ideologies, nationalism, often by violent means, furnishes the political unit and its system with legitimacy. … the nation state remains the main protector of cultural and physical security of people as well as the main distributor of cultural rewards and material resources.[35]

That position is likely to be reinforced by the actions of nationalists who see in social policy the option to reinforce national solidarity. Béland and Lecours comment: 'Social policy can be treated and articulated by nationalist leaders as symbols of a wider set of values, social priorities, and political culture. It also represents a tangible manifestation of the existence of a political community.'[36]

Some accounts of social policy are suspicious of an emphasis on the nation.[37] The concept is liable to be exclusive – the relationship of the nation state to outsiders in general, and migrants in particular, is a case in point. Titmuss's apprehension about the idea of a 'welfare state' was founded in part on a concern that the term could be used to limit responsibilities beyond national boundaries.[38] National cultures can be ethnocentric; some are racialised. Beyond that, nationalism has been associated with some of the most unpleasant manifestations of collectivism, including fascism and militarism. Harris's reference to 'violent means' points to the double-edged character of the concept. The history of independence and nation building in the twentieth century has not been a happy one. Many new states have been born out of civil strife – the states of the former Yugoslavia are an example. The development of nation states has routinely led to the displacement of millions of people, euphemistically referred to as 'population transfer': for example, up to 14 million Germans had to move after 1945, and about 10 million Hindus and Muslims exchanged between India and Pakistan. The road to liberation and independence has often been marked with violence.

---

[35] Harris, 2009, p 35.
[36] Béland, Lecours, 2008, p 24.
[37] e.g. F Williams, 1989, *Social policy*, Brighton: Polity.
[38] R Titmuss, 1968, *Commitment to welfare*, London: Allen and Unwin, p 127.

Despite those reservations, the positive aspects of the national community – citizenship, solidarity and inclusion – remain important. The ideas and practice of universality, rights or social justice have developed within bounded states. In the contemporary world, Paul Collier argues, countries commonly try to form a national identity as part of building a sense of common social responsibility and mutual commitment. 'Good' nationalism is inclusive: it is about forging a sense of community, of social obligation, about bringing people together.[39] Solidarity might be represented in terms of sentiment, but it is neither primarily subjective, nor emotional; it is based in bonds that develop through myriad small connections, obligations, practice and experience. 'The nation is defined', Zoe Williams argues, 'not by its puffed-up declaration of values, nor by its tacit cultural exclusions, but by what it built together and what it seeks to build.'[40] A common history and identity are not to be despised; they are part of the story of how those relationships come to be.

---

[39] P Collier, 2015, Good and bad nationalism, Social Europe, https://www. socialeurope.eu/nationalism, last obtained 28 September 2018.

[40] Z Williams, 2018, Nationalism can be a good thing, *Guardian*, 8 May, https:// www.theguardian.com/commentisfree/2018/may/08/nationalism-positive-case-immigration-counter-narrative-nhs, last obtained 28 September 2018.

PART II

Collective action for the common good

The elementary difference between collective and individual action is that in collective action, people do things together. Collective action is defined, not by what is to be done, but by how the group goes about it. Some of the reasons for collective action are principled; some are pragmatic; some are merely conventional, because the practice of collective action is long established. In the course of Part I, I have pointed to a range of circumstances in which things might be done individually or collectively. Collective provision often begins with a limited, partial pooling of resources and effort, and gradually expands as people come to think that collective action is, after all, a better way of doing things. This is a process, rather than a vision of society; there is a constant interplay between alternatives, and frequent shifts in balance and approach.

Having said that, the practice of collective action, and the character of provision made, tend in their turn to influence how things are done more generally, and the kinds of things that people want their services to do. The interpretation of core principles such as freedom or equality differs when groups, rather than individuals, are the focus. Democratic deliberation, voice and empowerment become the expectation and practice of public services; cooperation, working together, sharing and solidarity come to be seen as virtues in themselves. The second part of this book reviews the ways in which these different elements have suffused the idea of a common weal.

PART II

Collective action for the common good

6

Government and collective action

The nature of government

There is some confusion, in the literature, between the very idea of collective action and the role of government – an assumption that if people are calling for collective action, they must be calling for governments to intervene. When Dicey, the English legal theorist, wrote about the transition from individualism to collectivism, he was concerned almost wholly with the growth of government regulation and action. Collectivism meant 'the school of opinion often termed (and generally by more or less hostile critics) socialism, which favours the intervention of the State, even at some sacrifice of individual freedom, for the purpose of conferring benefit upon the mass of the people',[1] For Talcott Parsons, a polity was 'the aspect of all action concerned with the function of the collective pursuit of collective goals. ... collectivities are always the *agencies* of specific performances of societal function'.[2] The identification of collective action with political structures reflects a view that was widely held for much of the twentieth century. It makes sense, if policy is to be made at the level of a political community or a society, to invest the role of making policy in the formal structure of a government. But collectivism is not exclusively, or even primarily, concerned with macrosocial issues, and government is not the only, or even the most common, example of collective action in everyday life.

Government is a collective organisation of a special kind. It is difficult to define government in terms of the things it does – its functions – because in social policy, the same things are often done

---

[1] A Dicey, 1917, *Lectures on the relation between law and public opinion in England during the nineteenth century*, Lecture 4, http://oll.libertyfund.org/titles/dicey-lectures-on-the-relation-between-law-and-public-opinion-lf-ed, last obtained 28 September 2018.

[2] T Parsons, 1969 The political aspect of social structure and process, in *Politics and social structure*, New York: Free Press, p 318.

by non-state organisations. For example, social care can be provided by government, local government, commercially, by the voluntary sector, or by families. The provision of pensions in a welfare state might come from government and taxation; it might come from quasi-autonomous national bodies or funds; it might be based in a 'corporatist' arrangement, where government directs the operation of a nominally independent body;[3] it may be decentralised, through local government or autonomous units such as a health fund or a pensions fund; or it may be shared between government and a range of independent providers, potentially including mutual aid societies, commercial firms, employers and trade unions. Many developed countries have a three-tier system: independent contributory provision, a basic state scheme and social assistance for those who are not covered otherwise.

Given the difficulty of trying to describe an impossibly complex set of structures – 'governance' rather than 'government' – it helps to work from a generalised model, and then to vary the terms to accommodate differences in different countries. The starting point for a discussion of government is the idea of 'sovereignty'. The idea of sovereignty is often confused in popular discourse with a range of other issues – such as independence, self-determination, autonomy and control – but the main importance of the concept rests in something else. All legitimate government relies on the 'rule of law'. Law depends on there being a source of authority; the name of that source is sovereignty. In contemporary democracies, the source of authority is often supposed to be the sovereign 'people', but the precise character of the source of authority is not important for practical purposes – it may be a popular vote, a monarch, a parliamentary or presidential system, a constitution. There has to be a clear mechanism by which authority can be identified. In the United States, the source of authority is the Constitution. In the United Kingdom, the source is Parliament.

The rule of law means that all rules, all conduct by government, have to be authorised and carried out with due process. That runs much deeper than a statement that they are 'subject to authority' – the actions of government have to be authorised before any action can be taken, not just open to guidance after the event, and exercised consistently with that authority. The power of any official or set of officials is necessarily subject to the general principle, that they have

---

[3]   See e.g. P Schmitter, 1979, Still the century of corporatism?, in P Schmitter, G Lehmbruch (eds) *Trends towards corporatist intermediation*, Beverly Hills, CA: Sage; M Harrison, 1984, *Corporatism and the welfare state*, Aldershot: Gower.

to have both prior authority to hold their position, and authority for their actions. Governments and government officials cannot legitimately act as individuals; stepping outside their roles means that they act beyond the limits of their authority. Hart identifies a series of 'secondary rules', meta-rules which govern how we know what the law is. All legal systems require rules of recognition, that is, rules which allow us to know that the rules are legal ones; rules of change, which make it possible to change laws subsequently; and rules of adjudication, so that disputes can be resolved.[4] Another way of describing the same functions would be to refer to constitutional, legislative and judicial elements of government. The 'government' of a country, such as a president, ministers, cabinet and civil service, is often described as an 'executive', but the central character of the executive in a constitutional government is that it is not a source of authority in its own right – it works through the delegation of authority and is subject to limitations by the other branches. (These processes are not unique to governments. They are also evident in the kinds of social structure discussed in the first chapter of this book – the process by which any corporate organisation is able to make collective decisions, or to take collective action. The principle of referring to authority and making authority explicit is an important part of the culture of voluntary organisations – partly because those organisations imitate the patterns adopted in business and government, but equally because, over very long periods of time, the processes followed in voluntary and religious institutions, such as delegation of authority, audit and accountability, found their way into both the structures of government and the development of corporate business.)

Any source of authority depends on a recognition of legitimacy, and the nature of legitimacy has been one of the central questions of political philosophy. Legitimacy does not come from a single person, or individual; mediaeval writers thought it might have come from divine authority, but as doubts grew about theocratic government or the divine right of kings, there were only collective responses left. For the best part of five hundred years, most writers who have looked at the question have answered it in those terms (with the obvious exception of those, like American libertarians, who think that all government is probably illegitimate[5]). The fictive 'social contract' favoured by Hobbes, Locke or Rousseau is not about just a lawgiver or a committee of interested

---

[4]   H Hart, 1961, *The concept of law*, Oxford: Oxford University Press.

[5]   e.g. M Rothbard, 1978, *For a new liberty*, Auburn AL: Ludwig von Mises Institute, p 47.

individuals writing the rules; it is about people creating institutions which are capable of exercising authority.[6] (That is as true of Locke as it is of the others. Locke is assumed by many commentators to be an individualist; but he posits two contracts, the first between individuals to become members of a society, the second between the members of a society and the government.[7]) Burke and Hume emphasise a different process, which is one of prescription and acceptance of established norms over time; but the result is still a collectivity, or in Burke's terms a 'partnership'.[8]

Governments are often represented as a coercive force. Trotsky believed that 'Every state is founded on force'; Max Weber wrote, in the same vein, that 'a state is a human community that (successfully) claims the monopoly of the legitimate use of physical force within a given territory.'[9] The first proposition is debatable – many modern states have been formed in the belief that they could escape from the kind of force which had formerly been used against them, and in the hope that self-determination would deliver the kind of prosperity that other independent nations have achieved. The second proposition is just plain wrong: the US Constitution specifically (and notoriously) reserves the ultimate use of force to the citizenry, and while Weber might be forgiven for seeing the imperial powers of Europe in this light, that constitutional provision was made long before Weber was writing. What is true is a lesser proposition, that force or coercion is one of the options that is open to states. It has the important effect of reinforcing the norms and expectations imposed by governments, but it is often (especially by liberal democracies) seen as a last resort.

Governments can work through compulsion; but, as we know from the experience of 20th-century governments that tried to do it, extensive compulsion is hard work, and even the most ruthless and single-minded regimes find it difficult to keep it up in practice. Compliance with the law has much more to do with the establishment of norms – the combination of rules, expectations and common patterns of behaviour – than it does with sanctions. Laws are used to create a framework for managing people's affairs in normal life. At the heart of a legal system, there is constitutional law – not just the law

[6] E Barker (ed) 1971, *Social contract*, Oxford: Oxford University Press.

[7] J Locke, 1690, *Two treatises of civil government*, New York: Mentor, 1965.

[8] E Burke, 1790, Reflections on the Revolution in France, in E Payne (ed) *Burke: Select works*, Oxford: Clarendon Press, 1892, vol 2, p 114.

[9] M Weber, Politics as a vocation, in H Gerth, C Wright Mills (eds) 1946, *From Max Weber*, Oxford: Oxford University Press.

of government itself, but establishment of a system for recognising, making and changing rules; defining powers; and establishing who has them. Then there are the rules themselves, rules such as criminal law, laws governing contracts, laws governing property or laws governing families. Administrative law is about the process of government, determining how government – and indeed how other corporate bodies – may act. And then there is the establishment of sanctions – rules about punishment, redress and correction, all subject to processes of adjudication and dispute resolution. People do not drive on a particular side of the road because they are constantly being threatened with a sanction for disobeying; they follow the convention because it makes everyone's life easier to have a convention, whatever it is. The same is true for rather more complex conventions, such as marriage, employment or the incorporation of a business. Compliance depends, if not on active cooperation, at least on passive acceptance, and a policy where neither of those conditions is true – for example, drug control or the restrictions on copying music – is not likely to be effective.

Although legal systems are underpinned by coercion, much of what they do works in other ways. The main elements of legal systems are constitutional – they determine institutional legitimacy and practice – and regulatory, creating a framework for social life through the definition of groups such as families and businesses. In social policy, the laws relating to administration and delivery of the public services are especially important. Governments have also to work within the constraints of the constitutional and administrative systems they create – that is part of what the 'rule of law' means. Because governments have the authority to regulate the conduct of others in society, both individual and collective groups, they may be able to negotiate or bargain with others in order to co-opt them into process of implementing policy. They can regulate, restrict, promote or provide, offer rewards or impose penalties. Many European governments work on corporatist principles, seeking to delegate the role of government and incorporating other agencies into the government's purposes. Liberal governments, which are reluctant to intervene or coerce people directly, tend to prefer the options of trying to persuade, promote or educate people into desired patterns of behaviour.

Governments have come to play a major part in economic development, developing, financing and managing initiatives.[10] They also provide services directly; they are major employers, and often they

---

[10]   M Mazzucato, 2011, *The entrepreneurial state*, London: Demos.

are a driving force behind the public services. With more than two thirds of public spending being devoted to social welfare services or transfer payments, Minouche Shafik has argued, 'the state' has largely come to mean the welfare state.[11] Dicey commented on the growing trend to collective action in the English legal system:

> The practical man, oblivious or contemptuous of any theory of the social organism or general principles of social organisation, has been forced, by the necessities of the time, into an ever-deepening collectivist channel. Socialism, of course, he still rejects and despises. The individualist town councillor will walk along the municipal pavement, lit by municipal gas, and cleansed by municipal brooms with municipal water, and seeing, by the municipal clock in the municipal market, that he is too early to meet his children coming from the municipal school, hard by the county lunatic asylum and municipal hospital, will use the national telegraph system to tell them not to walk through the municipal park, but to come by the municipal tramway, to meet him in the municipal reading-room, by the municipal art gallery, museum, and library, where he intends to consult some of the national publications in order to prepare his next speech in the municipal town hall, in favour of the nationalisation of canals and the increase of Government control over the railway system. 'Socialism, Sir,' he will say, 'don't waste the time of a practical man by your fantastic absurdities. Self-help, Sir, individual self-help, that's what's made our city what it is.'[12]

There are critics who argue that government is illegitimate precisely because it is collectivist. The 'New Right', so-called,[13] object that all actions taken by government must in their nature limit the scope of individual liberty.[14] (The position is hardly 'new': Dicey recognised, and seemed to approve of, attempts to block public health vaccination

---

[11]   M Shafik, 2017, Beveridge 2.0: Rethinking the Welfare State for the 21st Century, London School of Economics lecture,www.lse.ac.uk/Events/2017/11/20171129t1830vLSE/beveridge, obtained 17 December 2017.

[12]   Dicey, 1917, Lecture 8.

[13]   N Barry, 1987, The new right, Beckenham: Croom Helm.

[14]   F Hayek, 1960, The constitution of liberty, London: Routledge and Kegan Paul; Rothbard, 1978.

or factory legislation in the name of individualism.[15]) I have examined libertarian arguments in some depth in my previous work: their central weakness has been their failure to distinguish legitimate from illegitimate intervention.[16] Some interventions may limit liberty, but others (such as the education of children) enhance it. Some actions taken by government are voluntary or permissive. The same collective action, such as the provision of public housing outlined in Box 6.1, would be legitimate if it were carried out by a voluntary organisation. The neoliberal objection seems to boil down to the idea that governments should not do anything that is legitimately authorised because they might go on to do something has not been authorised, and that is an argument for never doing anything. If a morally legitimate decision is made through a lawful, accountable process, it is difficult to see why there should be any moral objection.

At the other end of the political spectrum, there are the arguments of anarchists. There is no single species of anarchism, but one of its recurring themes is the argument that government exercises power in the interests of specific people, whether they are individuals or groups, at the expense of others.[17] There are different kinds of argument lurking under this – it can be difficult to tell whether it is a condemnation of the way that government operates, or the good faith of governments, or an intrinsic flaw in the model of legitimacy and accountability. Governments might fairly be criticised for their policy, or the morality of what they do, or their economic competence, or the way they go about things; but none of that does anything to distinguish collective action by government from any other sort of action. Unless we want to agree at the outset that every action taken by government is intrinsically illegitimate, it is difficult to say anything specific about the contribution of collective institutions and processes.

Government as collective action

In one sense, all government policies are collective: they are made through a collective process, on behalf of a political community. But that way of putting things would not distinguish collective policies from

---

[15] Dicey, 1917, Introduction to the second edition, section D, and Lecture 7.

[16] P Spicker, 2006, *Liberty, equality, fraternity*, Bristol: Policy Press.

[17] R Sylvan, 1993, Anarchism, in R Goodin, P Pettit (eds) *A companion to contemporary political philosophy*, Oxford: Blackwell.

any other kind of policy. It matters more that policies are conceived collectively, deal with collective groups and at times deal with people as if they were dealing with a collective. Government acts collectively:

- to regulate or shape the conduct of individuals: for example, through the operation of criminal law, or the use of incentives and disincentives to encourage specific behaviours;
- by dealing with broad categories of people as if they were also collective groups;
- to regulate or shape the conduct of groups, promoting collective action, or leading others to act collectively: for example, through actions to enhance culture or to promote public health;
- in its own right: for example, the collective provision of social services. Box 6.1 considers the particular example of the provision of housing by local government.

I have tried to distinguish moral and social issues from collective ones; but if government takes any moral or social position, that can be seen as collective action, too.

Box 6.1: Council housing: housing as a social service

Most contemporary discussions of housing policy treat it as if housing is a market commodity; for the most part, that is how housing is developed and allocated. Housing is individuated – it is usually sold or distributed user by user – and commoditised (sold or rented on the market for a price). In economic terms, however, housing is a very imperfect market – it suffers from the domination of a few major players, heavy reliance on credit allocation, market closure, market volatility (only a limited number of houses are on the market at any one time), the critical importance of location, imperfect information and externalities.[18] Many of these characteristics are impossible to avoid.

In this light, it is important to recognise that markets are not the whole story, and an alternative account is also possible: the development of housing as a social service. Council housing in the UK had its origins in the late 19th century. Councils had acquired substantial responsibilities for slum clearance

---

[18] J Barlow, S Duncan, 1994, *Success and failure in housing provision*, Oxford: Pergamon, ch 1.

in the 1870s, and after 1890 a limited number of properties were built by local authorities which saw the development as a corollary of slum clearance. After the First World War, policy shifted towards mass housing, 'housing for the working classes'; the kinds of justification that were canvassed included concern about the willingness of Glasgow workers to undermine the war effort by a rent strike, the need to avoid a Bolshevik revolution and the commitment to provide 'homes fit for heroes'. After 1930, the emphasis shifted more strongly towards slum clearance; by 1939, more than a million more council houses had been built. Major building programmes, in tandem with urban redevelopment and slum clearance, added another four million by 1970. Although another 1.4 million houses were built in the sector before 1985, the rate of housebuilding slowed, subsidies were gradually withdrawn, and over the course of the next 30 years much of the stock was sold or transferred from the control of local authorities to housing associations. This process has implied a degree of 'residualisation': social housing is liable to be seen as providing facilities for people with particular needs, rather than mass housing.

The reasons for the decline of council housing after that time have more to do with growing individualism, and a strongly held political view that housing might be better distributed by market criteria. That is not the subject here. Council housing in the UK has occupied several roles: the key roles have been public health, the provision of mass housing, and (in the 1970s and '80s) a more residual focus on social needs. All three of those roles are collective, but they are collective in different ways. Public health and slum clearance (the principal theme in the 1930s) worked partly by establishing minimum standards, but also by the removal of slums across broadly designated areas. The rationale for engagement in mass housing (especially in the 1950s and 60s) was founded in a view that people would be adequately housed only through government action to build and provide for the population. The 1951 Conservative Party Manifesto declared:

> Housing is the first of the social services. It is also one of the keys to increased productivity. Work, family life, health and education are all undermined by crowded houses. Therefore, a Conservative and Unionist Government will give housing a priority second only to national defence.

Provision for special needs, such as provision for homeless people, the needs of frail older people or people with disabilities, was emphasised much more strongly in the 1970s and '80s. It implied a more individuated service, but there is still a strong element of methodological collectivism: provision was planned collectively for segments of the population who are subsequently assessed on an individual basis in order to have the resources allocated. Subsequently, council housing has been run down, and its role has increasingly been passed to independent social housing providers.

Describing housing as a social service has three main implications. First, it implies a degree of collective organisation: there is some kind of institutional arrangement made to ensure its delivery. Second, there is some degree of collective distribution. All social services are redistributive: people who pay are not the same as people who benefit. Beyond that, social services tend to carry the implication that there is an element of dependency, that service users would otherwise be unable to provide the service from their own resources. Third, and perhaps more fundamentally, the idea of a social service implies that there is something essential – central, necessary and particularly important – about the issue being provided for. Housing has a key role in people's welfare, partly because it is vital in its own right, partly because it is the base from which so much else follows – issues such as warmth, sanitation, food preparation and much of the rest of modern living depend on it partly because housing is also a location, on which every other service depends. It is not really surprising that housing became central to many debates about welfare; if anything, it is more surprising that it has so widely ceased to be treated in that way.

If a government is responsible for everyone in a society, it becomes hard to justify a policy which is highly individuated – that is, a policy which deals with people one by one. When commercial insurers offer protection from risks, most of them differentiate according to people's personal circumstances: the premiums they charge are related to the risks assessed for each prospective insured person, and they are likely to make the terms for some high-risk individuals prohibitive – a process of 'adverse selection'.[19] When governments protect people from risks, they need to approach the issues differently; they have both to include people they have obligations towards, and to consider the risks for the whole population. It is not unusual for some government policies to fail to cover those risks – this is a general problem with policies that rely on market provision, because policies which give private firms a choice as to what to provide inevitably leave a residuum which is not otherwise covered. Wherever that is true, however, the governments in question have usually found themselves under pressure to fill the gaps.[20] The gradual movement to the comprehensive coverage of hospital care

---

[19] N Barr, 2004, *The economics of the welfare state*, Oxford: Oxford University Press.
[20] P Spicker, 2000, *The welfare state: A general theory*, London: Sage.

in developed countries is one example;[21] the rapid growth of social protection schemes in developing countries is another.[22]

The issues are often represented, in discussions of social policy, as lying between 'universal' and 'selective' social services. A universal approach applies, not necessarily to everyone, but to a category of people – children, older people, women and so on. Selectivity depends on a selection being made between those who are eligible and those who are not – typically a test of means or need. That may sound more individualistic, because such tests tend to be applied at the individual level, but selectivity is too broadly constructed to be individualised. In recent years there has been greater emphasis on 'personalisation', or adaptation of the service provided to the individual circumstances, needs and preferences of the service user. It is possible to think of universality and selectivity, not as polar opposites, but as a range of positions on a spectrum, moving from the most individualised policies to the least.

True individualisation is still uncommon. Laws that relate only to specific individuals or firms – referred to in the UK as 'Local and Personal Acts' or 'Private Acts' – do get passed, but they are uncommon. Methodological collectivism is so extensively used in government that it is almost a default position; the simple truth is that most government policies tend to deal with groups and categories of people, not with individuals. Part of this is about convenience, because governments are dealing with large numbers of people, but the difference runs deeper than that: dealing with large numbers of people leads to a different kind of perspective, a matter of dealing with waves rather than particles. Dealing with issues like economic growth or social mobility – both aggregate concepts covering a huge range of personal interactions – calls for governments to take an overview, and to deal with issues in general terms.

Government and civil society

Mainstream interpretations of the welfare state have often emphasised the importance and centrality of government action; but social policy has more typically begun with arrangements that were independent from government. Some of those arrangements were philanthropic or religious; some were communal. Where they could, people formed

---

[21] See V Paris, E Hewlett, A Auraaen, J Alexa, 2016, *Health care coverage in OECD countries in 2012*, OECD Health Working Papers No. 88, Paris: OECD Publishing, http://dx.doi.org/10.1787/5jlz3kbf7pzv-en, last obtained 28 September 2018.

[22] A Barrientos, D Hulme, 2009, Social protection for the poor and poorest in developing countries, *Oxford Development Studies* 37 (4) 439–56.

associations for mutual support, typically covering the risks of ill health and old age. In some countries, that kind of mutual support was based in guilds or trades unions, and in different places, unions had a major role in the provision of benefits, health care or housing.

In almost every case, governments have had to develop social policy, not with a blank sheet, but by considering their relationship with the pre-existing institutions. Some have gone about it by dismantling the old arrangements (as England did in Tudor times); some have tried to act as if existing arrangements no longer mattered (as Communist Poland did with the Catholic Church); others have tried to build on those arrangements, using state provision to do what existing arrangements did not (the principle followed in France). Governments have commonly intervened to expand the scope and coverage of policy; compulsion has mainly been used to extend provision to lower-income groups who might otherwise be excluded. In the Scandinavian countries, arrangements were commonly voluntary until the 1990s. In the US, health care is provided by a complex range of public, private, non-profit and mutualist organisations. The state provision of health care within that system is much broader than commonly understood, but it is easy to forget, in the heat of the debate, that millions of people are already covered through voluntary arrangements.

The idea of a unitary welfare state, where government accepts the primary or exclusive responsibility for the provision of services, bears little relationship to the practice and delivery of services. There is a 'mixed economy' of welfare, and governments typically operate within a complex network of services. Some governments have emphasised a 'corporatist' view, aiming to ensure that the range of services is complementary and coordinated; others have actively promoted complexity, in the belief that competition and diversity promote efficient service delivery. Box 6.2 focuses on the particular circumstances where governments have attempted to promote liberal markets based on competitive commercial services.

Box 6.2: Competition in public services

The New Right has argued that free markets are the best way to organise economic production and distribution.[23] The influence of free-market thinking has been widespread, and this kind of policy – associated with 'liberalisation',

---

[23] N P Barry, 1987; D S King, 1987, *The new right*, Basingstoke: Macmillan.

'structural adjustment' and marketisation – has been widespread in many different contexts.[24] The promotion of competition in the provision of public services is not the most important measure of the kind, but it illustrates something distinctive about the role of government within a neoliberal model: if government is going to be limited, it must be government that sets the rules and procedures in place to do it. Hayek argued that one of the principal roles of government is to create conditions where markets might be able to operate effectively.[25] Government has to go beyond regulation, and beyond withdrawal from the market, so as to establish a framework for competitive market provision.

In the European Union, there is a general presumption in favour of encouraging markets and competition:

> Any aid granted by a Member State or through State resources in any form whatsoever which distorts or threatens to distort competition by favouring certain undertakings or the production of certain goods shall, in so far as it affects trade between Member States, be incompatible with the common market.[26]

The Treaty of Rome, however, refers to 'services of general economic interest', which are 'market services which the Member States subject to specific public service obligations by virtue of a general interest criterion'.[27] The provision initially seemed to be aimed mainly at public utilities – telecommunications, postal services, transport, electricity and broadcasting – but the growth of market-based initiatives in pensions, education and health care have widened its scope. In a further communication in 2001, the European Commission emphasised that the rules in the Treaty only applied to services of general *economic* interest, and the Treaty did not apply to other fields such as education and social security provision.[28] Nevertheless, these are also areas where commercial providers could and do operate. The extension of the single market to cover public procurement issues opened up the possibility that traditional public services, like police or prisons, and social services, such as education or employability training, could be commodified and marketised.

---

[24] H Glennerster, J Midgley (eds) 1991, *The radical right and the welfare state*, Brighton: Harvester Wheatsheaf; C Gore, 2000, The rise and fall of the Washington Consensus as a paradigm for developing countries, *World Development* 28 (5) 789–804.

[25] See C Guest, 1997, Hayek on government: two views or one?, *History of Economics Review* 26 51–67.

[26] European Union, 2009, Treaty on the Functioning of the European Union (Lisbon Treaty), art 107; formerly art 87 of the Treaty on European Union.

[27] Com (96) 443 final.

[28] OJ 2001/C 17/04.

There has been a string of judgments in the European Court of Justice about different spheres of activity. The Commission has summed them up in two main categories[29] – but both categories rely on some rather obscure turns of phrase. The first category includes activities linked to the 'prerogatives' of the state: examples include policing, aviation control, prisons, railway infrastructure and measures to protect the environment. The second category consists of 'purely social' activities: examples include compulsory insurance and education. In the absence of any firm guiding principles, the conclusion seems to be that it all depends on context, and it is hard to say whether a service is economic or noneconomic; we are supposed to know it when we see it.

Introducing competition in public service provision is supposed to have many benefits, including lowering costs, developing choice, promoting innovation and improving service quality.[30] Competitive private provision is supposed to hold down costs and improve efficiency. It holds down costs because competition forces prices down, and if prices cannot be controlled, the returns to a business can then only be increased by lowering costs. It improves efficiency because firms are then constrained to produce at the lowest possible cost per unit.

The problem with this argument is that it only relates to part of any market. Private providers hold costs down, not just by doing things well, but by choosing what to produce, where to do it and who to do it for. They are efficient because they can avoid activities which drive up their unit costs; if activities are too expensive, competition will constrain them not to do them. Public services do not have those options. The arguments for choice, innovation and service quality are vaguer than the arguments for efficiency; there are certainly circumstances in which firms compete for custom by making offers about choice and quality, but it is unclear whether public services or social services are among them. In practice, the supply of such services tends to be short, choices are constrained and information is limited.[31]

Competitive systems present problems for the public services. Wherever there is competition, public and private systems adopt different roles. The effect of selection or producer choice is that there will be something left over – a residuum – and government, as the provider of last resort, has to make up the difference. The scope of government activity is determined by the hole that is

---

[29] Com (2003) 270.

[30] e.g. UK Office of Fair Trading, 2010, *Choice and competition in public services*, http://webarchive.nationalarchives.gov.uk/20140402165057/ http://oft.gov.uk/shared_oft/business_leaflets/general/oft1214.pdf, last obtained 28 September 2018; Cm 8145, 2011, *Open Public Services White Paper*, London: HM Government.

[31] See e.g. C Needham, 2011, *Personalising public services*, Bristol: Policy Press.

left after other services have been delivered; that is not necessarily well defined, or well chosen, or convenient. Typically the residuum is complex, dispersed and difficult to deal with. So it is hardly surprising if the public services appear at times to be expensive and fraught with difficulty: that is the consequence of giving them a residual role. It appears, then, that the model begins with an article of faith about the relative inferiority and inadequacy of state provision, and then acts to bring about the conditions in which that will be true.

The lines that separate government from civil society are often blurred, because governments have the authority to set the terms on which other organisations operate, and because the role of contemporary governments has led to their activities being interwoven with other independent and quasi-independent organisations. In welfare provision, there is a 'mixed economy' of welfare, where regulation, finance and production are all subject to multiple lines of influence and authority. Table 6.1 is taken from my book *Social Policy*.[32]

It can be difficult, in practice, to separate out what governments do from independent and voluntary provision: various systems in continental Europe are operated by quasi-autonomous bodies, or on a licence, or by organisations set up initially by government. States fund charities, and charities raise money for government activities. One of the ways of describing this kind of interrelationship has been 'corporatism', which tends to imply that government takes a lead, hierarchically, in planning and orchestrating the work of other organisations. Another way of seeing it is 'welfare pluralism', where there is a constant interplay of influences and so that no single actor can be said to be pre-eminent. International organisations have strongly emphasised the importance of 'partnerships' between actors – typically the state, nongovernmental organisations, private enterprise and the international agencies themselves; governments in developing countries have had to accept that they are not necessarily dominant actors within the framework.

This points to a paradox at the heart of many discussions of collective action. Government is a form of collective action, and there is often an assumption that an argument for considering collective action is more or less the same thing as a call for government action. At the same time, many of the arguments for collective action – arguments based on community, cooperation, solidarity, empowerment or inclusion – call for a different kind of response, a response that is likely to be

---

[32] P Spicker, 2014, *Social Policy: Theory and practice*, Bristol: Policy Press, p 257.

Table 6.1: The mixed economy of welfare

Finance	Provision				
	Public	Private	Voluntary	Mutual aid	Informal
Public	Social services departments	Private homes for elderly people	Delegated agency services	State-sponsored mutualist regimes	Foster care
Private corporate		Occupational welfare	Philanthropic foundations	Employer-sponsored workers' organisations	
Charges to consumers	Residential care for elderly people	Private health care	Housing association rents	Building societies	Child-minding
Mutualist (subscriptions/ contributions)	National insurance	Health Maintenance Organis-ations		Union pension funds	
Voluntary	Hospital friends	Purchase of services by voluntary organisations	Religious welfare organisations	Self-help groups	Family care

communitarian, pluralistic and diverse. It may well be that the way to promote collective action and mutual responsibility is not to depend on the actions of government, but to let independent organisations, communities and social networks do things differently.

Democratic government

'Democracy' means many things. There is a wide range of idealised or theoretical constructions of the idea, such as the 'sovereignty of the people', the 'popular will' or liberal democracy. Then there are institutional accounts, based on voting and elections, political participation or representative government. And then there are accounts which identify democracy with a set of principles — accountability, human rights and the rule of law. For many people, democracy goes beyond politics: it offers economic prosperity, social inclusion and personal development.[33]

The identification of democracy with government 'by the people', or even of the 'will of the people', depends on a certain type of collectivist construction: it sees 'the people' as a construct that is capable of governing, or of having a will. A common objection to collectivism denies that collective units can do anything, but I have already dealt with that argument: a business, an institution or a committee are examples of ways that people can and do act collectively. For collective institutions to act, however, people within the institution have to have roles. Any collective interpretation of democratic government is implicitly based on the idea that people do have such roles — typically as 'voters' or 'citizens'. Some of the political science literature does little to distinguish those two categories, and treats the act of voting as the primary form of political participation.[34] In other literature, participation is much more concerned with engagement in decision making.[35] Voting is not a very good indicator of that — partly because it is done so infrequently, partly because so many elections around the world are rigged, or for a single candidate.

In a representative democracy, the roles are relatively well defined. Electors vote for representatives, representatives form the basis on which the legislature or executive is formed, and the actions of the representatives are shaped by the constitutional arrangements of the

---

[33] P Spicker, 2008, Government for the people, *International Journal of Social Welfare* 17 251–9.

[34] G Almond, S Verba, 1963, *The civic culture*, Boston, MA: Little, Brown.

[35] e.g. A Richardson, 1983, *Participation*, London: RKP.

system they have been selected to serve in. In a participative or 'direct' democracy, the situation is much less clear. The central implication of direct democracy is that each citizen potentially has a role in decision making. That begs the obvious question: how?

There are two main resolutions. One is voting on specific issues, following a settled convention where decisions are made by a majority of voters. Counting heads, James Fitzjames Stephen once wrote, is better than breaking them.[36] One of the critical safeguards of 'liberal democracy' is the protection of the rights of minorities; without such rights, there is always the potential for majority interests to dominate. I reviewed, however, an argument for considering the position of voters earlier. The argument is based on the position taken by Madison in the *Federalist Papers*. A majority is simply a coalition of interests – a combination of minorities;[37] it cannot be legitimate to override people's rights when they are in a majority if it would not be if they were in a minority.

The second resolution is the 'republican' model, in principle modelled on the republics of ancient Greece or Rome. Quentin Skinner has commented that its advocates treated classical texts as if they had 'an almost wholly unproblematic relevance to their own circumstances'.[38] Rousseau imagined a community where the people assembled in a body in order to deliberate and discuss issues which could be decided by popular acclaim. He seems to have thought that city states could still have been run on these lines in the 18th century.[39] For most of the intervening period, the idea of direct democracy has looked to be hopelessly unrealistic, but quite suddenly – it is a development of the last 15 years – there is a technology to do it: people from round the world have animated discussions in online forums. The virtues of this technology are clear: immediate communication, sharing information and evidence, and public transparency. So, however, are its vices. There are no rules, and the medium seems to favour extremism, intemperance and lack of thought.[40]

---

[36] J F Stephen, 1874, *Liberty, equality, fraternity*, Chicago, IL: University of Chicago Press, 1990, p 28.

[37] J Madison, 1788, *Federalist Papers 51*, New York: Mentor, 1961, p 311.

[38] Q Skinner, 1996, cited in S Glover, 1999, *The Putney debates, Past and Present* 164 47–80, p 54.

[39] J-J Rousseau, 1762, *Du contrat social*, III i.

[40] See *The Guardian*, 2017, What is covfefe?, 31 May, https://www.theguardian.com/us-news/2017/may/31/what-is-covfefe-donald-trump-baffles-twitter-post, last obtained 28 September 2018.

There are dangers in the idea of direct democracy, of which more shortly, but there is also a powerful case for engaging the citizenry in the discussion of issues. The central character of democracy, Joshua Cohen has argued, is based on 'deliberation'[41] – government through a process of sharing and comparing competing views. Among the most important features of democracy, Sen argues, is openness and the ability to criticise – that is one of the reasons why a free press is so important.[42] The model of 'radical democracy' is a fusion of participative and deliberative approaches; it is a process for extending deliberation.[43] Direct democracy, or civic engagement in the political process, is one of the ways that can be done – not the only way, but an important one nevertheless.

---

[41] J Cohen, 1997, Deliberation and democratic legitimacy, in R Goodin, P Pettit (eds) *Contemporary political philosophy*, Oxford: Blackwell.

[42] See e.g. A Sen, 2001, *Development as freedom*, Oxford: Oxford University Press.

[43] J Cohen, A Fung, 2004, Radical democracy, *Swiss Political Science Review* 10 (4) 23–34.

7

Radical democracy

Civic republicanism

'Civic republicanism' refers to a set of collectivist approaches based on active engagement in a political community. Bill Jordan identifies the republican tradition with Aristotle. There are five key elements:

'1. A political community is a shared project ... every polis (or state) is a species of association ...

2. The people who join together to form a political community have a bond to each other. ...

3. The political community aims to achieve the common good of its members. ...

4. Membership of a political community (citizenship) is an active, not a passive process: the members must rule themselves. ...

5. Power used to activate commitment to the common good is self-rule, the collective ability to achieve the goals of the community.'[1]

The 'republican' label was popularised in the 1970s and '80s, but the terms of the discourse are very old. The foundations of the American republic had been attributed to the influence of John Locke and possessive individualism, but historians identified, beyond that, a different strand in the revolutionary movement, associated with the ideas of the mediaeval guilds, Machiavelli, the Levellers and the English Civil War.[2] In a world where the structure of power had been determined primarily in terms of duties and obligations to one's superiors, those who wanted to oppose those structures tended to do so by looking for a different source of legitimacy, resting in the power of the people. In the discourse of republicanism, government

---

[1] B Jordan, 1989, *The common good*, Oxford: Blackwell, pp 69–70.

[2] D Rodgers, 1992, Republicanism: the career of a concept, *Journal of American History* 79 (1) 11–38.

depends on the citizenry, who form a concept of the common good and mandate their government to pursue it.

There are parallels in contemporary politics; people looking for a radical, participative democracy are drawing on the same principles. Habermas distinguishes 'liberalism' from 'radical democracy' in these terms:

> Liberals begin with the legal institutionalization of equal liberties, conceiving these as rights held by individual subjects. In their view, human rights enjoy normative priority over democracy, and the constitutional separation of powers has priority over the will of the democratic legislature. Advocates of egalitarianism, on the other hand, conceive the collective practice of free and equal persons as sovereign will-formation. They understand human rights as an expression of the sovereign will of the people, and the constitutional separation of powers emerges from the enlightened will of the democratic legislature.[3]

Either model might be compatible with republicanism, but the key elements of civic republicanism lean more to the latter than the former.

Honohan identifies several key strands in republican thought: a common good, citizenship, civic virtue and freedom.[4] In Rousseau's thought, the idea of a common good was linked to a general will: everyone wanted what was good for everyone. He distinguished the general will from the will of all; the general will is not an aggregate set of decisions, but a collective one. That meant, of course, that the general will had to be distinguished from the sort of things that people actually said. Rousseau suggested looking for the broad consensus within a range of views;[5] later revolutionary movements saw the task of finding the true general will as the role of a benign popular leadership. It has been true in the past, and there are still examples in the present, that some repressive movements claim to speak for 'the people' as a whole. I will come back to the idea of a common good in due course.

Second, there is the main point emphasised by Jordan: citizenship and active engagement in a political community, usually expressed in

---

[3] J Habermas, 1988, Popular sovereignty as procedure, in J Bohman, W Rehg (eds) 1997, *Deliberative democracy*, Cambridge, MA: MIT Press, p 44.

[4] I Honohan, 2002, *Civic republicanism*, London: Routledge.

[5] J-J Rousseau, 1762, *Du contrat social*, book II, ch 3.

terms of political participation. The arguments for active engagement are strong, but the nature of the political community in radical democracy is often idealised. Titmuss wrote, 'All collectively provided services are deliberately designed to meet certain socially recognised needs; they are manifestations ... of society's will to survive as an organic whole.'[6] The organic metaphor can be taken too far. Some mediaeval views of society were corporate, seeing it as a body; fascists and idealists wrote about 'social surgery', cutting out the diseased parts of society to cure the whole. Treating society as a global, overarching unit sets up an opposition between the interests of individuals and their society; it treats a society as a remote, distant and often oppressive monolith. It is questionable whether it is meaningful to talk about 'society' as having a 'will to survive', or treating it as a unified entity. What may be more true is that there is, at the global level, a political community: an elected government, a locus of authority or sovereignty, a level at which laws are made. For some, the political community – stereotypically, the nation state – is the level at which the common good is expressed: one expression used in foreign policy is the 'national interest'. It is liable to be judged by the success of the economy, or the influence of a country in the world, but it could as easily be expressed in terms of the 'people's home' (*folkshemmet*) or the common weal.

The role of the political community is justified partly in terms of these moral interrelationships, but also by pursuing legitimacy through collective action and consent. One of the principal objections to the idea of a 'common good' is a matter of process and procedure: how can we find out what it is? Who should we ask, and what do we do with the answers? We can consult the citizenry, but many views are not necessarily collective ones, and what is good for many is not necessarily good for all. Within the republican tradition, these problems are addressed by political engagement and participative democracy. Part of this relates to the concept of freedom, and the emphasis on self-determination, of which more shortly; part to an emphasis on the responsibility of the citizen; but there was no less a value attached to democracy in the classical sense, as a source of legitimacy and a means of arriving at consensus about the common good. There is a deep ambiguity in republican views of the polity. On one hand, there are those who look to the polity as the basis for shared values, shared

---

[6] R Titmuss, 1955, The social division of welfare, in *Essays on 'the welfare state'*, London: Allen and Unwin, 1963, p 39.

perceptions and political agreement. If the purpose of the polity is to pursue a common good, including the common weal or the promotion of social cohesion, it seems to call for the resolution – or even the avoidance – of conflict. Rousseau thought that implied a relatively small society,[7] like that of his native Geneva, where everyone (or at least, everyone bar women and servants) could participate in decision making. On the other, there are those who see the political community in terms of radical pluralism, based on difference, diversity and the rights of minorities; the whole purpose of a political community is to make it possible to develop some collective action that is compatible with those differences. Implicit in the idea of citizenship there is an assumption of civic equality, in which each member of the political community occupies the status of a citizen.

The third element is a strong belief in civic virtue, and a parallel emphasis on moral action in the public interest. Much of the literature on the idea of civic virtue has focused on the virtues that are appropriate for a liberal democracy (in general) and the United States in particular; there is a longstanding debate within liberalism as to whether markets and reliance on self-interest can be seen as a guarantee of appropriate conduct, or whether further qualities are needed. Dagger identifies three core values inherent in the idea of civic virtue.[8] They are the avoidance of corruption – the subordination of private gain to the benefit of the community; the avoidance of dependence, because it undermines the capacity of the citizen for self-determination; and the assertion of liberty, through participation in political decision making.[9] As he develops the argument, he tends to move towards a 'thicker' concept of the virtues: they include education, active engagement in civic affairs, recognition of the rights of others, enshrined in the rule of law, and – less predictably – engagement in the 'civic memory', a sense of culture, heritage and common enterprise. Galston goes further, identifying a fully developed, or 'thick', set of virtues that are looked for in a democracy: general virtues, such as law-abidingness and courage; social virtues, such as independence and tolerance; economic virtues, including a work ethic and flexibility; and political virtues, including respect of other people's rights and engagement in dialogue, and more specifically virtues of leadership where required.[10] The 'virtue' of civic

---

[7] Rousseau, 1762, Book III, pi.

[8] R Dagger, 1997, *Civic virtues*, Oxford: Oxford University Press.

[9] Dagger, 1997, pp 14–15.

[10] W Galston, 1988, Liberal virtues, *American Political Science Review* 82 (4) 1277–90.

republicanism is by contrast a relatively undeveloped or 'thin' concept. The republicans understood that public and private interests were different things, and made it the object of the republic to promote the public interest. Virtue consisted partly in the sacrifice of the personal to the collective, and partly in ethical conduct.

There is a recurrent emphasis in contemporary policy documents on issues of ethics and 'leadership', but this is a questionable basis for safeguards; emphasising the ethical role of leaders does too little to guarantee rights, minority interests or abuses of power. The American republicans were rooted in this tradition, but this is one of the key issues where they departed markedly from other republican conventions: their scepticism about the motives of those in power led them to frame the constitution deliberately to restrain the scope for government action, guaranteeing legal redress, 'checks and balances'.

The fourth main element of republicanism is a belief in freedom. This is usually expressed in simple terms: to be free, the people had to be subject to no masters. The conventional representation of freedom is based on judgments about people's actions. The literature focuses mainly on the distinction between 'negative' freedom, the absence of restraint, from 'positive' freedom, the power or capacity to act. The two concepts overlap: all free action, Maccallum argues, is the freedom of a person, from restraint, to do something.[11] In the republican tradition, however, freedom is not about action at all. Freedom is a status: people are free, or not free.[12] In ancient Rome, the central distinction made between people was that some were citizens, some were free men, and some were slaves. In modern terms, we tend to think of the issue of slavery as being about ownership, but that is not how it would mainly have been conceived for much of the pre-modern period. A slave or a serf was attached to a household, or to the land; they were the 'subject' of the person who was responsible for that estate. And being 'subject' meant that they were bound by the decisions of a master – the head of household, or the lord. A woman was subject to the power of a man, a servant to a master, a member of the household to the head of the household, a serf to a lord. One of the contexts in which 'domination' and 'dependency' are most often seen together in contemporary discourse is in the discussion of economic development, where dependency theory has been influential

---

[11] G Maccallum, 1967, Negative and positive freedom, *Philosophical Review*, 76 312–34.

[12] P Pettit, 2008, Republican freedom: three axioms, four theorems, in C Laborde and J Maynor (eds) *Republicanism and political theory*, Oxford: Blackwell.

in Latin America;[13] the issues are outlined in Box 7.1. The republican approach has considerable limitations, but it is important to recognise how often the concerns of the left – Mandela's 'long walk to freedom', resistance to imperialism, freedom for the Palestinian people – build on this ancient model.

Box 7.1: Independence, neocolonialism and structural dependency

Many countries which had been colonies of the major empires became independent in the period after the Second World War. Another wave followed with the collapse of Communism and the breakup of the Soviet Union. But the trend towards the formation of nation states was visible long before. Belgium, notoriously the colonial power responsible for the Congo, had itself been a colony of Spain before the French Revolution. The rise of Napoleon broke the lines of communication, and it formally became independent in 1821. It later became, notoriously, a colonial power in its own right. The Haitian republic of 1804, taking at face value some of the arguments made during the French Revolution, was rewarded for its rebellion by being subject to penal compensation, including reparations for the loss of slaves. Haiti, now one of the poorest countries on earth, continued to make these payments to France until 1947.[14]

The core argument for independence was the same argument found in civic republicanism: that a nation was not free if it was subject to the will of a master. Independence was self-determination. Unfortunately, many of the newly independent nations continued to suffer major problems, high levels of indebtedness and exploitation of their assets by established property holders. One of the sources of continuing poverty is the 'natural resources' trap:[15] an abundance of resources attracts a certain kind of business, more concerned with extracting wealth than with human development. In many former colonies and poorer countries, the problems were attributed to global capitalism: a combination of exploitation, rigged trade rules, indebtedness and military force has acted to continue their subjugation. Some writers on development, such as Andre Gunder Frank, have argued that some of the middle-ranked countries of South America

---

[13] e.g. A Gunder Frank, 2014, The development of underdevelopment, in M Seligson and J Passé-Smith, *Development and underdevelopment*, Boulder, CO: Rienner, ch 23.

[14] A Phillips, 2008, Haiti, France and the independence debt of 1825, Vancouver: Canada Haiti Action Network, https://canada-haiti.ca/sites/default/files/Haiti,%20 France%20and%20the%20Independence%20Debt%20of%201825_0.pdf, last obtained 28 September 2018.

[15] P Collier, 2007, *The bottom billion*, Oxford: Oxford University Press, ch 3.

have become 'structurally dependent' on more developed economies, locked into a situation of permanent economic disadvantage.[16]

If we are looking for reasons why many newly independent countries have done badly, there are so many that it becomes difficult to distinguish them. The first, and simplest reason is that they were doing badly before. Poverty is not a trap: if it was, Collier argues, no country would ever escape from it.[17] However, moving from poverty and limited economic capacity calls for a massive change in economics and society. There has to be an infrastructure, including basic issues such as water, roads, energy supply, and places for people to live.

The second reason is that there are obstacles to development. Collier points to a range of problems: armed conflict, geography (mainly being landlocked with bad neighbours), overreliance on natural resources (because that distracts industry from developing productive capacity) and bad government. Corruption plays an important part – a reason for poverty as well as a consequence of it.

And then there is the behaviour of other countries, particularly of richer countries. Singer and Ansari point to the unequal distribution of military power, financial and economic influence and resources, industry, commerce, food security and the influence of multinational corporations.[18] The rules for international trade are heavily rigged in favour of richer countries – they demand free trade for their products, but deny entry to exports from poor countries.[19] The international organisations have to some extent reinforced the disadvantage of poor countries by imposing free market rules, in the form of 'structural adjustment'. Structural adjustment did not lead to the benefits that were expected of it, and the evaluations are full of excuses as to why not.[20] Later policies, which encouraged governments and the organisations in civil society to form their own policies, have been much more successful.

Populism

The ideas that infuse radical democracy have recently come to the fore in one of the major political movements of our time: the rise of

---

[16] Gunder Frank, 2014.

[17] Collier, 2007, p 5.

[18] H Singer, J Ansari, 1992, *Rich and poor countries*, London: Routledge, p 12.

[19] Make Trade Fair, 2002, *Rigged rules and double standards*, Oxford: Oxfam International.

[20] D Dollar, J Svensson, 2000, What explains the success or failure of Structural Adjustment Programmes?, *Economic Journal* 10 894–917.

populism. Populism – 'the people versus the powerful'[21] – is not always coherent, and often not coherently presented; that makes it easy to dismiss the trend as a cry of anger. For some, populism is a style of argument rather than a substantive ideology.[22] For others, populism is a strategy based on charismatic leadership of disaffected individuals.[23] Populist parties (and populist politicians) have flourished in recent years by appealing to the marginalised and the disaffected. Decker writes:

> Populist parties and movements are a product of modernization crises in society. They emerge when, in the wake of excessively rapid change or dramatic upheavals, particular sections of the population see their values being eroded, or suffer disorientation. This sense of loss, which may have economic causes, but is normally generated by cultural factors, is accompanied by a fear of declining status, uncertainty about the future and feelings of political alienation.[24]

However, populism is much more than a chorus of complaint. The definitions of the term offered by academic writers are generally consistent with each other:

> an ideology that considers society to be ultimately separated into two homogeneous and antagonistic groups, 'the pure people' versus 'the corrupt elite', and which argues that politics should be an expression of the volonté générale (general will) of the people.[25]

This use of the *volonté générale* comes directly from Rousseau: 'The general will is always right and always tends to the public benefit… The people is never corrupted, but often it is deceived.'[26] Populism, in the same spirit, is

---

[21] e.g. P James, 2004, The people versus the powerful, *Guardian*, 5 February.

[22] E Laclau, 2005, Populism: what's in a name?, in F Panizza (ed) *Populism and the mirror of democracy*, London: Verso.

[23] N Gidron, B Bonikowski, 2013, *Varieties of populism*, Cambridge, MA: Weatherhead Center, Harvard.

[24] F Decker, 2008, Germany, in D Albertazzi, D McDonnell (eds) *Twenty-first century populism*, Basingstoke: Palgrave Macmillan, p 122.

[25] C Mudde, 2004, The populist zeitgeist, *Government and Opposition* 39 (4) 541–63.

[26] J-J Rousseau, 1762, *Du contrat social*, Book II, ch. 3.

an ideology which pits a virtuous and homogeneous people against a set of elites and dangerous 'others' who are together depicted as depriving (or attempting to deprive) the sovereign people of their rights, values, prosperity, identity and voice.[27]

The central element of populism is a focus on 'the people'. 'The people' is possibly a political community, possibly a society, possibly a community of identity. Taggart suggests that populism does not necessarily refer to conventional understandings of a political community, such as the nation; there tends to be emphasis on an emotional core, which he terms the 'heartland', 'a construction of the good life derived retrospectively from a romanticized conception of life as it has been lived'.[28] The position was expressed with some force in the British referendum on the European Union: 'I want my country back.'[29] If the people are not 'homogeneous', a term also used in several accounts,[30] they certainly share at least common values and common purposes. Populists claim that the views they represent are the views of 'the people' – that is where the label of populism comes from. Opposing the will of the people is characterised as antidemocratic, illegitimate (of course) and evidence of allying oneself with the forces that stand against the people.

The second theme is the restoration of sovereignty to the people, which in terms of direct democracy, implies conformity with the people's will. The conventional procedures of representative democracy are often taken to be an obstruction to the exercise of popular sovereignty (which is why judges of the High Court, deciding that the necessary authorities had not been obtained by the government preparing for leaving the European Community, were denounced in the press as 'enemies of the people'[31]).

---

[27] Albertazzi, McDonnell, 2008, p 34.

[28] P Taggart, 2000, *Populism*, Buckingham: Open University Press, ch 8; P Taggart, 2003, *The populist turn in the politics of the new Europe*, Brighton: University of Sussex, p 11.

[29] See R Foster, 2016, 'I want my country back': the resurgence of English nationalism, http://blogs.lse.ac.uk/brexit/2016/09/06/i-want-my-country-back-the-resurgence-of-english-nationalism, last obtained 28 September 2018.

[30] K Abts, S Rummens, 2007, Populism versus democracy, *Political Studies* 55 405–424.

[31] See C Phipps, 2016, British newspapers react to judges' Brexit ruling, *Guardian*, 4 November, https://www.theguardian.com/politics/2016/nov/04/enemies-of-the-people-british-newspapers-react-judges-brexit-ruling, last obtained 28 September 2018.

The third is the attitude to elites, those in power or the 'establishment'. For Abts and Rummens, populism is defined by the antagonism of the people towards the elite.[32] We have had too much of experts; we have to drain the swamp.[33] The establishment and the elite are flexible terms which it seems can be extended to include academics, intellectuals, managers, lawyers and selected politicians. The leaders of the populist movements – from recent populist rhetoric in the US and UK, billionaires, property magnates and stockbrokers – appear to be exempt from the general structures on elite management, because they are enacting the will of the people.

That leads directly to the fourth point, which is about leadership. 'The leader and party/movement', Albertazzi and McDonnell write, 'are one with the people'.[34] This is not the sort of 'leader' found in evangelical books on management, where inspirational individuals motivate their followers to change in unexpected directions. The leader of a populist movement is the voice of the people, who expresses the general will of the people.

Box 7.2 gives the example of a radical populist movement, *La Via Campesina*, which argues for 'food sovereignty' in developing economies.

Box 7.2: Food sovereignty

La Via Campesina is an international anticapitalist movement. This is from their website:

> For too many years, we have witnessed with deep pain the systematic plunder and destruction of our precious natural resources and the oppression of our people. We know that our African elites in the public and private sectors have been for many years colluding in corruption with the evil transnational corporations which today represent the new face of imperialist neo-colonialism. We are appalled by this and demand an immediate end to immoral and irresponsible behaviour of many of our leaders.[35]

---

[32] Abts, Rummens, 2007.

[33] See *Financial Times*, 2016, Britain has had enough of experts, says Gove, https://www.ft.com/content/3be49734-29cb-11e6-83e4-abc22d5d108c, last obtained 28 September 2018; *Washington Post*, 2018, Trump promised to drain the swamp, https://www.youtube.com/watch?v=Gg9ypxT9V3g, last obtained 28 September 2018.

[34] Albertazzi, McDonnell, 2008, p 7.

[35] Via Campesina, 2007, Declaration of Nyeleni, https://nyeleni.org/spip.php?article290, last obtained 28 September 2018.

This message is fundamentally populist; it represents a virtuous people opposed by an oppressive elite. The oppressors are not the farmers, the local businesses or the men of high status in a community (they are usually men);[36] they are multinational corporations and agribusinesses.

The movement 'defends small-scale sustainable peasant agriculture as a way to promote social justice and dignity based on food sovereignty'. Food sovereignty is explained in these terms:

> Food sovereignty is the right of peoples to healthy and culturally appropriate food produced through ecologically sound and sustainable methods, and their right to define their own food and agriculture systems. It puts the aspirations and needs of those who produce, distribute and consume food at the heart of food systems and policies rather than the demands of markets and corporations.[37]

There are good arguments for mutuality, cooperation and community action in development. The core elements of cooperative industry are 'industrial democracy' and joint ownership.[38] The paradigmatic example is Mondragon in the Basque country. Food sovereignty, however, is not a proposal for cooperative agricultural production; it is an argument for shifting power to local communities. It proposes to do that by making communities much more self-reliant.

The first problem with food sovereignty is that self-reliance makes people vulnerable – that is, it limits their ability to cope with harm. Food sovereignty cannot offer a response to problems like civil war, drought or climate change. If (or when) such things happen, the localities where they happen will be not be protected by a system that is relatively localised. On the contrary, localisation makes poor communities more vulnerable to such events.

Second, providing healthy diets locally and on a small scale must mean less food. That is true partly because it is only possible to provide varied diets locally by growing things that grow less well locally along with those that grow better. If the local area is suited to growing coffee, for example, diverting production away from coffee to produce fruit and vegetables – which are essential for any

---

[36] See H White, R Menon, H Waddington, 2018, *Community-driven development: Does it build social cohesion or infrastructure?*, International Initiative for Impact Evaluation, www.3ieimpact.org/media/filer_public/2018/03/12/wp30-cdd.pdf, last obtained 28 September 2018.

[37] Via Campesina, 2007.

[38] R Oakeshott, *The case for workers' coops*, Basingstoke: Macmillan, 1990.

healthy diet – means that compromises have to be made. The other part of the loss is attributable to the restriction of trade. Localism restricts the division of labour, and consequently it limits the scope for cooperation.

Third, there are the problems of control and exclusion. Communities define insiders and outsiders; the process is exclusive as well as inclusive. Localism excludes people. People get left out, shut out or pushed out. Some flee; that has traditionally been one of the factors leading to urbanisation.

Fourth, food sovereignty does no address distributive issues at a local level. Food sovereignty does not create, develop or guarantee that people will get what they need to eat. If the entitlements are held by the producers, or by local community organisations, they are not held by each and every individual.

The idea of food sovereignty threatens, then, to make existing problems worse. Food security depends on people having food to eat. Local control and self-sufficiency is not the way to make people more secure; it is likely to do the opposite.

Populism and radical democracy

'Populism', Hayward writes, 'lays claim not merely to being democratic but to embodying the most authentic version of democracy'.[39] Populism may not be what civic republicans and the advocates of radical democracy have in mind, but it offers a very close fit. The first section of this chapter identified five key elements in radical democracy; all of them are present in populist movements.

The first element is about citizenship. Citizenship and membership of the political community are identified in populism with 'the people'. Populists are not always clear who 'the people' are, but they are much clearer about who they are not, and migrants and members of minority ethnic groups do not usually make the cut. This is perfectly consistent with citizenship, because membership of a community is liable to be exclusive as well as inclusive.

Next there is the expression of the common good. In the populist model, as in Rousseau's political thought, this is translated into the terms of the general will[40] – the general will is the way for the people's

---

[39] J Hayward, 1996, *The populist challenge to elitist democracy in Europe*, Oxford: Oxford University Press, p 10.
[40] J-J Rousseau, 1762, in Barker, 1971, book II.

aspiration for the common good to be chosen. Opposition to the general will is then equivalent to opposition to the good of the people.

The third element in the populist narrative is civic virtue. The people, Albertazzi and McDonnell write, are inherently good. They are variously described as 'virtuous' or 'pure', by contrast with the rotten establishment.[41]

The idea of engagement in the political community is the idea that seems to undergo the greatest transformation in the process of translation. Populist mistrust of the conventional elements of liberal democracy – the electoral process, the representative government, the rule of law – implies some distance between political participation and popular involvement. Populism has often been characterised by frustration with the slow and awkward processes associated with deliberative democracy. Protest can be communicated through ballot boxes, but also through rallies, street demonstration and possibly direct action, such as President Duterte's murderous forays against drug dealers in the Philippines, or Donald Trump's invitation to 'Second Amendment people'[42] – that is, people with guns – to resist. (The Second Amendment may seem in itself to represent a major departure from the model of democratic deliberation, but it was explicitly identified in the US constitution as a necessary protection against tyranny.)

The same antagonism is manifest in the interpretation of freedom from domination. The dominators are generally the elite, the establishment, though, depending on context and circumstances, it is not difficult to extend that resentment to bankers or the institutions of the European Union.

Populism is not just something that looks a bit like the model of radical democracy, or something that bears a tangential relationship. It is a paradigmatic example of civic republicanism in practice, subject only to minor embellishments. Chantal Mouffe has suggested that populism is inherent in democracy, and that reference to popular sovereignty is an important corrective to the dominance of liberal discourses. Her main concern is not with those who claim to speak for the people, but with the political content of right-wing claims.[43] One of the characteristic features of contemporary populism is not inherent in any definition of the idea: it

---

[41] Albertazzi, McDonnell 2008, p 6.

[42] N Corasaniti, M Haberman, 2016, Donald Trump suggests 'Second Amendment people could act against Hillary Clinton', *New York Times* www.nytimes.com/2016/08/10/us/politics/donald-trump-hillary-clinton.html, last obtained 28 September 2018.

[43] C Mouffe, 2005, The 'end of politics' and the challenge of right wing populism, in F Panniza (ed) *Populism and the mirror of democracy*, London: Verso.

is the denial of the validity of any opposing view. But that, too, can be justified by a belief that the people are uniquely the source of legitimacy. Saul Alinsky, a radical advocate of community organisation, had a decided taste for confrontation rather than negotiation. He explained:

> if your function is to attack apathy and get people to participate it is necessary to attack the prevailing patterns of organized living in the community. The first step in community organization is community disorganization. The disruption of the present organization is the first step toward community organization. Present arrangements must be disorganized if they are to be displaced by new patterns that provide the opportunities and means for citizen participation. All change means disorganization of the old and organization of the new.[44]

Alinsky tells us: 'Pick the target, freeze it, personalize it, and polarize it.'[45] It is a small step from the left-wing Alinksy to the 'alt-right', or – as several commentators in the American press have recognised – to the tactics of President Trump.[46] Many of the beliefs and approaches that radicals have embraced – empowerment, non-domination, civic virtue, opposition to elites and collective action for the common good – have a dark side, a potential for abuse that is intrinsic to the way that the concepts have been formed. Without the necessary safeguards, the will of the people can become an instrument of oppression. We rely on external values, such as human rights, freedom, equality, rights of assembly, free speech and the rule of law, to moderate the process of collective action.

Habermas's characterisation of radical democracy leaves no room for such safeguards. He consistently emphasises the importance of communication as a foundation for ethical conduct, and he is apparently

---

[44] S Alinsky, 1989, *Rules for radicals*, New York: Random House, p 112.

[45] Alinksy, 1989, p 124.

[46] M Bargo, 2016, Trump's leadership style in Alinskyan perspective, www.americanthinker.com/articles/2016/08/trumps_leadership_style_in_alinskyan_perspective.html, last obtained 28 September 2018; M Barone, 2016, Trump uses Saul Alinsky tactics against Alinsky acolyte Clinton, www.washingtonexaminer.com/trump-uses-saul-alinsky-tactics-against-alinsky-acolyte-clinton/article/2603237, last obtained 28 September 2018; H Fineman, 2016, Saul Alinsky had nothing but contempt for the system – who does that remind you of?, *Huffington Post*, www.huffingtonpost.com/entry/donald-trump-saul-alinsky_us_578fd95de4b0bdddc4d2e280, last obtained 28 September 2018.

convinced that an effective process of deliberation, founded on principles, will yield legitimate outcomes, and in itself offer protection from illegitimate decisions.[47] At the beginning of this chapter, I offered a lengthy quotation by him, and it is now time to revisit it. Habermas describes radical democracy in terms that are nakedly populist. He writes that 'Advocates of egalitarianism … understand human rights as an expression of the sovereign will of the people.' That grants the will of the people a sovereign status, above and beyond any conception of rights. Treating human rights as subordinate to the general will, whether or not that is developed communicatively, invites the obvious corollary that the general will can override them. Then he redefines the purpose and practice of equality. There may be those of us who think that the plea for equality has something to do with rights, or justice, or human dignity. Not a bit of it. The expression of equality, according to Habermas, is about something quite different: 'Advocates of egalitarianism … conceive the collective practice of free and equal persons as sovereign will-formation.' Finally, the purpose and product of radical democracy is not the promotion of values such as freedom and equality, but the expression of the will of the people. It follows that those who oppose the will of the people – most obviously in the defence of minorities – are not truly egalitarian, because real egalitarians respect the will of the people.

If legitimacy comes entirely from the will of the people, it becomes possible to ignore the character of what is being done. We have seen a great deal of this sort of argument from other populists recently. Habermas's defence of this position seems to be that he should not be taken too literally: 'the normative tension between equality and liberty can be resolved as soon as one renounces an overly concrete reading of the principle of popular sovereignty.'[48] If this is intended to deflect critics from close scrutiny, it does not work. At best, Habermas's characterisation of radical democracy is a mistake. At worst, it is a threat to the values that he claims to hold.

---

[47] D Munro, 2007, Norms, motives and radical democracy, *Journal of Political Philosophy* 15 (4) 447–72.

[48] J Habermas, 1988, pp 47–8.

8

Collective values

An emphasis on radical democracy may give the impression that collectivism is a doctrine of the left. It may look that way, but collective approaches appear in types and shades of political opinion across the spectrum. The range of collective approaches is far from uniform; the term stretches from conservatives to radicals, or authoritarians to anarchists. General terms such as 'socialism' or 'conservatism' cover a broad range of principles and perspectives, both individual and collective. Socialism is collective in the sense that it may refer to collective organisation of society, characteristically (but not always) in terms of class or social movements; to the extent that it promotes collective values, such as mutual aid, cooperation and solidarity; in the methods it favours, including radical democracy and state intervention; and in the interpretation of the values associated with socialism, such as equality and social justice. But it is individual in its emphasis on individual rights, human dignity and personal capacity. Conservatism is collective in its understanding of society as a partnership or common enterprise; its support for established institutions, including church and state; and its emphasis on social order, and the values of family, heritage and nation. It tends to be individualistic in its scepticism about its defence of property rights, its approach to economic policy and the protection of individual liberty.

Collectivism offers us a set of perspectives, rather than any specific political doctrine, and those perspectives inform a wide variety of political positions. Collectivist views might be held to include, for example,

- pluralism, which interprets politics in terms of the interplay of organised interest groups and multiple actors;
- institutionalism, which analyses political processes by looking at the interactions between formal institutions and society;[1]

---

[1]   V Schmidt, 2006, Institutionalism, in C Hay, M Lister, D Marsh (eds) *The state*, Basingstoke: Palgrave 2006; B G Peters, 2011, Institutional theory, in M Bevir (ed) *The Sage handbook of governance*, Los Angeles, CA: Sage.

- solidarism, which emphasises substantive collectivism, and the interaction in society of a multitude of diverse, overlapping supportive groups;[2]
- collectivist doctrines which focus on the relationships between particular aspects of society, like radical feminism (gender), Marxism (economic classes), nationalism (nations), or Hegelianism (states); and
- organic corporatism, which (in this sense) can mean that society or a nation is understood as if it were a body or organism.[3]

Box 8.1, considering some of the arguments for taxation and redistribution, unavoidably draws on the influence of a range of moral positions.

Despite the diversity of such views, it can probably be said that a collective mindset does tend to lead in a different direction from an individualist one. Thinking of people within the framework of collective relationships implies a different way of looking at values. Take, for example, the interpretation of 'freedom'. A goodly part of the literature on freedom comes at it from an individual perspective: a person is free if that person is not constrained and able to make choices.[4] There are variants within this, in particular the different emphases placed on lack of interference in a 'negative' view of freedom, on property rights and on the importance of choice, but the core of individualistic interpretations is the central figure of the autonomous, self-determining individual. People might be poor, or disabled, or homeless, but that does not mean they are not free, so long as they can make their own decisions.[5] People have rights to make their own choices and govern their own lives.

The position I have just outlined is not just individualistic; it is atomised, treating every actor as if they could be understood in isolation from every other actor. In any model of freedom where people are acting in concert with others, freedom is a matter of social relationships. That could be interpreted in many ways. One of those perspectives has been the republican account of freedom, considered in the previous chapter; freedom is concerned with the power to

---

[2] L Bourgeois, 1896, *Solidarisme*, Paris: Armand Colin.

[3] See e.g. H Spencer (1860), The social organism, www.econlib.org/library/LFBooks/Spencer/spnMvS9.html, last obtained 28 September 2018.

[4] See e.g. F Hayek, 1960, *The constitution of liberty*, London: Routledge and Kegan Paul; I Berlin, 1969, *Four essays on liberty*, Oxford: Oxford University Press.

[5] e.g. Berlin, 1969, p 122.

make decisions as a community. In contemporary socialism and social democracy, people's freedom depends on their capacity to act in that context, and the capacity of other people around them. Tawney, for example, wrote that 'Freedom is always relative to power.'[6] Where people are isolated, poor or excluded, they become less free; where the capacity of a group is limited, so is the freedom of the people within it. Freedom can be increased by increasing people's capacity, by giving people more resources, by empowerment and giving people the chance to influence political processes.

The same kind of shift in emphasis can be seen in understandings of equality. Equality is necessarily a social concept – it depends on a comparison with the situation of other people – but sometimes the comparisons are made between individuals, sometimes between groups. Concern about equality at the level of individuals tends to emphasise the equality of persons, that people should not have a status assigned to them at birth; equality of opportunity, taken as the opportunity to better oneself, the 'career open to the talents'; and citizenship, represented, for example, in the right to vote or equality before the law.[7] Collectivist approaches generally accept all of that, but many go further: expressing a view of opportunity that relies on a common material foundation, a view of citizenship that extends to social and economic rights, a redress in the imbalance of power, and some degree of equality of welfare, at least to the extent that people have basic security and conditions of life needed to allow them to live freely. Rae argues that the concepts of equality which arise once people start talking about groups of people are liable to find themselves in conflict with individualised accounts: 'bloc-regarding equality', looking at such issues as gender or race, leads in a different direction from 'individual-regarding' equality.[8] The idea of 'affirmative action', or positive discrimination, is difficult to justify from a purely individualistic point of view; it is concerned with changing relationships between social groups, such as minority ethnic groups, with the rest of society.

This, in turn, stretches to understandings of social justice. Where individualists accept the idea of social justice – not all do, and Hayek dismisses it as a 'mirage'[9] – it mainly refers to fair dealing, and sometimes to fair outcomes. By contrast, collectivist concepts of social justice are much broader: collectivists have taken the view, at different times, that

---

[6] R Tawney, 1931, *Equality*, London: Unwin, p 107.

[7] See P Spicker, 2006, *Liberty, equality, fraternity*, Bristol: Policy Press, ch 3.

[8] D Rae, 1981, *Equalities*, Cambridge, MA: Harvard University Press.

[9] F Hayek, 1976, *Law, legislation and liberty*, vol 2, Henley: Routledge and Kegan Paul.

social justice requires the redress of historic grievances, a degree of equality, a reallocation of social resources and substantial shifts in the distribution of power.

This constellation of values – liberty, equality and justice, and collective action – should be familiar. They are all identified with the great slogan of the French Revolution, 'liberty, equality, fraternity'. Taken in a collective sense, those values are closely identified with socialism, not a model of society but a set of beliefs standing for 'the principles of freedom, equality, solidarity, democracy, respect of Human Rights and Fundamental Freedoms, and respect for the Rule of Law'.[10] The traditions of social policy are partly those of the political left, which argued that it was possible to use social institutions to change social relationships. They were strongly influenced by a 'perfectionist' tradition, especially the 19th-century social reformers who believed that better social organisation was a route to the development of better people.[11] Christian socialism argued for moral responsibility, shared resources and communal action; the 'idealism' of the late 19th century emphasised 'corporate identity, individual altruism, ethical imperatives and active citizen-participation'.[12] As is often the case, that brings together a range of perspectives that might be individual or collective.

Collective action as a value in itself

Thinking about things collectively does not (or should not) imply a slavish acceptance of any form of collective action. There are aspects of collective life which can reasonably be valued, and others – notably those which interfere with individual autonomy and personal rights – which should not be. Criticisms of collective values tend to dwell on the implications for individuals, but to understand the force of these values they have to be seen in a collective perspective. There are three sorts of values to consider. First, collective action is seen as a value in itself – something to be promoted and cherished. Next, there are values which promote collective action, and make it possible to carry

---

[10]   See Party of European Socialists, 2015, PES Statutes, https://www.pes.eu/export/ sites/default/Downloads/PES-Documents/FINAL_amended_PES_Statutes_EN_ clean.pdf_64645215.pdf, last obtained 28 September 2018.

[11]   e.g. R Owen, 1813, *A new view of society*, London: Dent; O Hill, 1875, *Homes of the London poor*, London: Frank Cass.

[12]   J Harris, 1992, Political thought and the welfare state 1870–1940, *Past and Present* 135 116–41, p 137.

it out – values which make it possible for people to form groups, to identify with them and to take action along with others. Then there are some substantively collective values, such as 'culture' or 'defence', which can only be understood collectively.

Cooperation. There are good, self-interested reasons for people to cooperate with each other. People who cooperate can do things together with others that they cannot do by themselves. The division of labour is pervasive throughout contemporary society; it happens because it makes it possible for everyone to do more and to have more. But it is not possible to insist that people cooperate only for self-interested reasons, because groups such as families and tribes have existed long before there was any concept of modern society; living in groups is part of the human condition.

As a broad proposition, words about cooperation are positive: being cooperative, a good team player, able to share, unselfish, ready to pull one's weight. Words about people who are reluctant to cooperate are much less positive: self-interested, egocentric, uncooperative, rogue, loner. 'Self-sufficient' is probably neutral, and only a few terms – 'independently minded' or 'self-reliant' – have a positive ring (although, in fairness, Hollywood has built an industry on presenting such people in a positive light). The central point seems to be that collaborating with others is something to be approved of – without, apparently, first considering what people are working together to achieve.

The value which is attached to cooperation goes beyond any sense of rational benefit. This has some intriguing implications for values. Triandis reports evidence that cultures which are more oriented to collective values are likely to favour approaches which avoid or reduce conflict, such as mediation; cultures which stress individualism tend to prefer more formal justice, openness and direct confrontation.[13] Beyond the existence of cooperation in itself, effective collaborative action calls for negotiation and compromise. Those, too, are seen as virtues to be encouraged.

Social capital. The idea of social capital was introduced to address a gap in the discussion of 'human capital', which relates to individual skills and development. 'Social capital' is used to describe the value that people gain through having social systems that support them

---

[13] H Triandis, 2001, Individualism-collectivism and personality, *Journal of Personality* 6 (1) 907–24, p 909.

or provide amenities, which otherwise they may have to supply from their own resources. Social networks offer group activities, contacts, protection against risk and (in the case of families) real access to financial resources. For Coleman, who popularised the term, social capital is based mainly in two characteristics of such networks: trustworthiness and the extent of obligations that are held,[14] which might be identified with the principle of reciprocity,[15] considered below.

The idea of 'social capital' has proved popular in international organisations where discourse tends to be dominated by economists looking for valuations and measurement before any issue can be taken seriously. Social capital is not, strictly speaking, capital, and it is difficult to measure it in those terms. But there is a core truth lying behind the idea: that people who can draw on social networks have greater effective command over resources than those who do not. References to 'community capacity' are not empty: some communities have more resources and skills than others, and people living in those communities have an advantage over those who have no such base.[16]

Solidarity. The idea of solidarity is one of the central social values referred to in Europe, but the same term, 'solidarity', in English is often used in a much thinner and weaker sense. In English, solidarity is often taken to be a sentiment, characterised by fellow feeling – standing shoulder to shoulder with one's comrades. That is a pale shadow of what the term means in most of its contemporary uses. In the first place, solidarity is based on interdependency. Hartley Dean writes:

> human relationships and the interdependency they entail are a good in and of themselves ... interdependency is an essential feature of the human life course and the human condition. One might argue that it is constitutive of our humanity and the achievement of human identity.[17]

The relationships that bind a society are sometimes referred to as 'organic'. When Durkheim distinguished organic from mechanical

---

[14] J Coleman, 1988, Social capital in the creation of human capital, *American Journal of Sociology* 94 (Supplement) pp S95–S120.

[15] E Ostrom, T Ahn, 2003, *Foundations of social capital*, Cheltenham: Edward Elgar.

[16] D Narayan, R Chambers, M Shah, P Petesch, 2000, *Voices of the poor: Crying out for change*, New York: World Bank/Oxford University Press, ch 10.

[17] H Dean, 2004, Reconceptualising dependency, responsibility and rights, in H Dean (ed) *The Ethics of Welfare*, Bristol: Policy Press, pp 193–4.

solidarity, he was referring to the commonplace, everyday cooperative and collaborative relationships that people form.[18] Their 'organic' nature rests in the level, complexity and degree of integration of the interconnections between them. The organic view of society, favoured in traditional conservatism, saw both individual and social relationships in terms of established patterns of custom, behaviour and culture. Even Hayek, though he denied that any relationships beyond the individual had meaning, argued that 'true individualism' started from 'men whose whole nature and character is determined by their existence in society'.[19]

The idea of solidarity, however, goes beyond a recognition of social networks; it is as much a moral concept as an empirical one. Solidarity refers to a set of mutual responsibilities and commitments – the 'glue' which holds together social groups. In Catholic social teaching, solidarity is 'the good of all and of each individual, because we are all really responsible for each other'.[20] There is some idealism in the feeling that we might be able to extend this to everyone else, and it is not obvious that anyone ever does that (or should). As a general proposition, solidarity is particular rather than general. The closer the personal relations one has, the stronger the obligations are: that is how we know that they are close. National solidarity, where it exists, is built on the strengths of smaller, stronger networks.

Social cohesion. The idea of social cohesion might be seen as a way of looking at the common good – what is good for a society; but, as in the assumption that cooperation is a good thing, it seems to disregard what people are cohering for. Cohesion can sound like a mixed blessing, because some of the most cohesive societies historically – including caste societies, feudalism and theocracy – have also been some of the most oppressive. Contemporary conceptions of social cohesion put rather more emphasis on coexistence, collaboration and mutual support. The Council of Europe has identified a long series of definitions of social cohesion, for example:

> the promotion of stable, co-operative and sustainable communities;

---

[18]   E Durkheim, 1893, *De la division du travail social*, Paris: Alcan.
[19]   F Hayek, 1948, *Individualism and economic order*, Chicago, IL: University of Chicago Press, p 6.
[20]   Pope John Paul II, 1987, *Sollicitudo rei socialis*, Vatican: Catholic Church.

the ongoing process of developing a community of shared values;

a state of affairs in which a group of people ... demonstrate an aptitude for collaboration; or

the capacity of citizens living under different social or economic circumstances to live together in harmony.[21]

But the association of stability, harmony and peaceful coexistence elevates the principle to the status of a desirable end in itself.

Society as a common asset, joint enterprise or partnership. The last of the values to consider in this section has no generally accepted name or label. Sometimes it is collapsed into the idea of 'solidarity', or an idea that 'we are all in this together', but its influence extends beyond that. Everything that people do is affected by others. The members of a society may not work cooperatively, but we are interdependent. Without the efforts of other people – builders, engineers, doctors, police and so on – the things that people do, and the things they own, do not have the same value – and, indeed, many of them would be impossible. (The same idea is captured in the French construction of employers and trades unions as 'social partners'.) Property is not created, as libertarians imagine,[22] by the labour and independent efforts of isolated individuals; it is a social convention.

From there it is a small step to the radical idea that people collectively have a claim to resources that might otherwise be claimed by the few. Major Douglas argued that property and production depended on the community, and a 'cultural inheritance':

It is both pragmatically and ethically undeniable that the ownership of these intangible factors vests in the members of the living community, without distinction, as tenants-for-life. ... it is an inheritance from the labours of past generations of scientists, organisers, and administrators ... If this point of view be admitted, and I find it difficult to

---

[21] Council of Europe, 2005, *Concerted development of social cohesion indicators: Methodology guide,* Council of Europe.
[22] G Brennan, D Friedman, 1981, A libertarian perspective on welfare, in P G Brown, C Johnson, P Vernier (eds) *Income support: Conceptual and policy issues,* Totowa, NJ: Rowman and Littlefield, p 27.

believe that anyone who will consider the matter from an unprejudiced point of view can deny it, it seems clear that the money equivalent of this property, which is so important a factor in production, vests in and arises from the individuals who are the tenants-for-life of it.[23]

It followed that the people at large were entitled to a dividend from the value generated by a society. The argument for a 'Social Credit' (Douglas's term) or 'Social Dividend' became one of the cornerstones of the case for a Universal Basic Income.[24]

Box 8.1: Taxation and redistribution

Taxes are used to raise finance for government, but they do far more than that. They are also used to regulate the economy by injecting or withdrawing resources, to offer incentives and disincentives for particular actions, to reward or punish, to signal government intentions, to spread or allocate social costs, to equalise the position of different actors in the economy, to encourage or discourage relationships with other countries, and so on. In the specific context of a discussion of collective values, taxation also has a role. Taxes can be used, whether symbolically or in reality, to show that people are 'all in it together' – or the reverse, which is to offer privileges to some that are denied to others; to fund transfer payments, where money effectively goes from group of people to another; to fund services; or as a device for pooling risk, the basis of social protection.

Individualist 'libertarians' have deep reservations about taxation: they see taxes as the privation of a person's property. Taxation is theft; alternatively, some critics suggest, it is a form of slavery, because it effectively means that people are working not for themselves but for the government.[25] From a collectivist perspective, neither argument has merit. In the first place, property is based on a set of conventions, not on the individual production of commodities in splendid isolation. Monetary income in particular is very much a social construct. The conventions include some calculation of the taxes a person needs to pay: there is no reason to imagine that if there was not taxation, everyone would receive just the same pay cheque they do now. Then, even if one accepts that property

---

[23] C Douglas, 1933, Social credit, www.friendsofsabbath.org/Further_Research/e-books/Social_Credit.pdf, last obtained 28 September 2018, p 27.

[24] See e.g. A Downes, S Lansley (eds) 2018, *It's Basic Income*, Bristol: Policy Press.

[25] M Rothbard, 1978, *For a new liberty*, Auburn, AL: Ludwig von Mises Institute, p 29; R Nozick, 1974, *Anarchy state and utopia*, New York: Basic Books, p 169.

does attach to individuals in the way that libertarians claim, it does not follow that it is sacrosanct; there may be other priorities and issues to consider. The question that is likely to be asked by individualists opposed to redistributive taxation is, 'why should my money be used to support other people?' The first collectivist response is, 'what makes you think it's your money?'; the second is, 'why do you think your claim is stronger?' There is nowhere in the world where governments have not implicitly taken a collectivist view – but equally, there is almost certainly nowhere where some individual taxpayers have not felt they were justified in withholding tax on the basis that it was their own money. Some tax regimes allow individuals to divert tax expenditure to satisfy personal preferences for different kinds of communal activity.

Moving from taxation to redistribution is a small step. All collective services are individually redistributive, in the sense that those who pay are not necessarily the same as those who benefit. Mutual insurance is redistributive, moving funds from those who have not suffered harm to those who have. Building a road is redistributive, because the value that people draw from it will not be proportionate to the amount they pay. (That is an impossible thing to ask, and it would not be proportionate if it was provided for in a competitive market, either.) Pensions are redistributive, because people die at varying times. If funds raised through taxation are applied to any sort of provision, of pooled risk or direct transfer, there will be some element of redistribution.

That does not tell us, however, who wins and who loses. Not all redistribution is progressive, from richer people to poorer people. Much is horizontal – between categories of population, such as redistribution from adults to children, or from workers to pensioners. Some is regressive, moving from poorer people to richer ones. The implication of the preceding argument – that property is conventional and that redistribution follows from any collective effort – is that regressive redistribution may also be defensible. Examples are subsidies to industry, tax reliefs and incentives for investment – it all depends what the redistributive measure is trying to achieve. It is sometimes tempting to associate individualism with the political right wing, and collectivism with the political left; but there is no necessary association of collectivism with egalitarianism. There is a case to be made for egalitarian redistribution, but it relies on other principles beyond the distinction of individual and collective views of property.

Constitutive values

Social groups, it was explained earlier, have three main characteristics: identity, relationships between members (or between members and the group), and a capacity for common action. Some of the values considered in the previous section contribute to this, but groups have their own rationales and reasons for being. The associated values can be thought of as constitutive; they help to explain or justify group formation and continued membership.

Identity. It is not always the case that identifying with a group is portrayed in a favourable light, but being denied the scope to express one's identity is generally portrayed in a bad one. People have many identities, and not all of those identities are immediately relevant to group formation or collective action – identities of gender, disability, sexuality, education or occupation may or may not be relevant, depending on circumstances. (That comment may surprise some committed activists in those fields, because it does not square with their own experience – if it was not highly relevant to them, they would not be activists; but it is descriptive of a wider reality. These identities may, in context, be individual, rather than collective; they may be held without associating with a broader group; and they do not imply solidaristic relationships with others who have the same identity.)

Some identities, however, are associated with 'belonging' – that is, being a member of a definable group. There are identities that are formed because someone is identifying with a social group – for example, identities of culture, religious affiliation (as opposed to belief, which might be individual), nationality, employees or membership of a political party – and identity cannot be considered in isolation. For most of this book, I have used the term 'identity' in a particular context: the identity that attaches to groups. But there is also the identity of individuals, where people draw on the characteristics of groups to say something about themselves. People often treat identity as if it were also a moral status: people may be 'proud' to be American, Flemish-speaking, Jewish, gay, parents, female, lawyers, employees or conservatives (not all at the same time, of course), and they see their identities as cause for celebration. Identity is a source of pride and value. But it can be a source of social conflict, notably when pride in one identity makes a claim for superiority over others.

Reciprocity. The bonds of 'solidarity' are based less on altruism than on reciprocity and shared obligation. The most evident model is the example of family care, where there are complex, overlapping obligations between the parties: obligations of direct exchange, but also of generalised reciprocity (circles of exchange which are never complete); one of the ways we know that we are close to other people is that we do not demand the same level of immediate reciprocation that is looked for from strangers. Sahlins argues that families depend on generalised reciprocity; there is no place for a calculation of costs and benefits.[26] Various writers have seen this kind of generalised reciprocity as the basis for a stronger, mutually supportive society: Mauss identified his work on gifts with the development of social insurance,[27] and Titmuss identified the 'gift relationship' with the idea of welfare.[28]

Loyalty. Loyalty is used more broadly than for social groups alone – firms refer to 'customer loyalty' when they mean to refer to repeat business – but it is about consistency and commitment. In part it is associated with fidelity or keeping faith – a person who has committed to a particular relationship undertakes to meet the requirements of that relationship; in part it is about reciprocity, because people accept obligations to reciprocate as part of being part of a solidaristic network. It is another uncertain virtue, because its merits depend on what one is loyal to.

Shared purpose. Jordan's account of the republican tradition[29] or Habermas's advocacy of will formation[30] are expressive of a widely held belief: the sense that people can be part of something bigger than themselves; that this can help to affirm, validate and reinforce their personal objectives; that shared values are evidence of solidarity; that sharing values and aims with other people is a fine and noble thing. Like loyalty or cohesion, however, common purpose is also capable of being misdirected: it can be used to justify wars, ethnic conflict and the subjugation of other groups.

This can be linked with the concept of collective action as a joint enterprise or partnership, but they are not equivalent. One of the key elements of a social group is that people are brought into a relationship with others in the group. A shared purpose might be evidence of that kind of relationship – but it is not a guarantee in itself that such relationships have been formed, or that they will be.

Sharing a common purpose is an instrumental value for groups; it should help in principle to reduce conflict, enhance cooperation

---

[26] M Sahlins, 1974, *Stone age economics*, London: Tavistock.

[27] M Mauss, 1925, *The gift: Forms and functions of exchange in archaic societies*, London: Cohen and West.

[28] R M Titmuss, 1970, *The gift relationship*, Harmondsworth: Penguin.

[29] B Jordan, 1989, *The common good*, Oxford: Blackwell, pp 69–70.

[30] J Habermas, 1988, Popular sovereignty as procedure, and in J Bohman, W Rehg (eds) 1997, *Deliberative democracy*, Cambridge, MA: MIT Press, p 44.

and improve teamwork. People are expected to be 'on board' with each other, and 'leaders' are supposed to offer them a programme that will motivate them.[31] The literature on managing organisations raises questions about the validity of this approach. Too often, the aims that are specified are the wrong aims; the aims are too diverse, or they focus attention too narrowly; they are too challenging; the timing is wrong; organisations are pushed to take risks or to behave unethically.[32] From the perspective of social psychology, Brown suggests that the common-sense view, that group cohesion leads to better performance, probably has it backwards. In a longitudinal experiment of team performance, 'superior performance early on was correlated with subsequent cohesion, but initial cohesion was not reliably related to later performance'. Common purpose does seem to be more important empirically than whether people in a group get on with each other, but good performance has more effect than either.[33]

Substantively collective values

The values considered up to this point either value collective action as a good in its own right, or they support collectivism by justifying collective action. Principles such as cooperation and reciprocity encourage people to form groups and reinforce their identification with the groups when they have done so. Beyond this, there are also values which are at root collective in their nature, and a collectivist approach is implicit in any arguments relating to those values.

Stewardship. The principle of stewardship is often identified with environmental movements but is much broader than consideration of the environment alone.[34] There is a general expectation, within this model, that every generation tries to leave the world a better place for the generation which comes after it. The obligation to support future generations is there, in large part, because previous generations worked to the same principle, and we have a duty to do as much for future generations. People in society have obligations to the people

---

[31]   G Latham, 2011, Goal setting, in M Di Domenico, S Vangen, N Winchester, D Boojihawon, J Mordaunt (eds) *Organizational collaboration*, London: Routledge, ch 2.

[32]   L Ordonez, M Schweitzer, A Galinsky, M Bazerman, 2011, Goals gone wild: the systematic side effects of over-prescribing goal setting, in Domenico et al, ch 3.

[33]   R Brown, 2000, *Group processes*, Oxford: Blackwell, p 53.

[34]   J Passmore, 1974, *Man's responsibility for nature*, London: Duckworth, ch 2.

who have come before them, and to those who come after. Society, Edmund Burke wrote, is a partnership, not just of those who are living, but between those who are living, those who are dead and those who are yet to be born.[35] It is possible to see that as an organic view of society – perhaps even a metaphysical one – built on the constitutive principles of solidarity and reciprocity. People owe responsibilities to previous generations because of direct reciprocity: we are all, as children, raised by the previous generation, and that implies an obligation towards them. The same is true of the obligations of the next generation: parents raise children, and children have responsibility to parents. Direct reciprocity is only a part of the story, however. There is also a principle of generalised exchange – exchange that can never be complete. People look after parents (in part) because parents looked after their own parents; they look after their children (in part) because their parents looked after them. At a broader social level, pensioners are paid for not by their savings, but by the contributions of the working population; the working population expects, in turn, to be paid for by the generation that comes after it. They expect, in their turn, to be supported by the next generation.

Culture, heritage and tradition. 'Culture' is a very broad term; an important part of the idea of a culture is descriptive of patterns of behaviour and relationships, and there is an academic literature on cultural studies which has built its empire on the haughty view that all human activity is cultural. In its narrower sense, it can also be taken to refer to heritage, tradition and 'cultural life', and those are seen as values in their own right. The UN charters refer to participation in cultural life as a human right: 'The States Parties to the present Covenant recognize the right of everyone to take part in cultural life.'[36] UN documents tend to be vague about what that means, but for practical purposes we can take it to refer to engagement in social activities, such as language, music, art, leisure pursuits and ceremony, which are considered to express the nature of a society or a section of it. The implications of these principles for indigenous peoples, outlined in Box 8.2, are illustrative. Cultural rights are both individual and collective – they have to be enforceable at the level of the individual,

---

[35] E Burke, 1790, Reflections on the Revolution in France, in E Payne (ed) *Burke: Select works*, Oxford: Clarendon Press, 1892, vol 2, p 114.

[36] United Nations, 1966, International Covenant on Economic, Social and Cultural Rights, art 15, www.ohchr.org/EN/ProfessionalInterest/Pages/CESCR.aspx, last obtained 28 September 2018.

or individuals can be prevented from taking part – but the culture they refer to is collective. What is prized in a culture is what is shared with others – not least because it is shared with others. What is not shared has to be thought about in different terms, as a matter of personal choice, character or diversity.

Box 8.2: The rights of indigenous peoples

Rights govern the way that other people are supposed to behave towards the people who hold them. Most conventional representations of rights begin with the individual, but many of the arguments that hold for individuals – rights relating to protection from exploitation or violence, human development and basic security – might also apply to groups. That position is accepted in relation to juridical persons, such as companies or trusts, but it needs to be extended beyond that to other sorts of social group.

There are some 300 million people in the world who can be considered to be members of indigenous minorities in the countries where they live. They are likely to have lower income, poorer health and lower life expectancy than the rest of the population.[37] The United Nations adopted its Declaration on the Rights of Indigenous Peoples in 2007.[38] The declaration promises rights to maintain a culture, to protection of religious traditions and to maintenance of minority languages. It states, among many other things, that

> States shall provide effective mechanisms for prevention of, and redress for:
> (a) Any action which has the aim or effect of depriving them of their integrity as distinct peoples, or of their cultural values or ethnic identities;
> (b) Any action which has the aim or effect of dispossessing them of their lands, territories or resources;
> (c) Any form of forced population transfer which has the aim or effect of violating or undermining any of their rights;
> (d) Any form of forced assimilation or integration;
> (e) Any form of propaganda designed to promote or incite racial or ethnic discrimination directed against them.

---

[37] R Eversole, J McNeish, A Cimadamore (eds) 2005, *Indigenous peoples and poverty*, London: CROP/Zed.

[38] United Nations, 2007, Declaration on the Rights of Indigenous Peoples, www.un.org/esa/socdev/unpfii/documents/DRIPS_en.pdf, last obtained 28 September 2018.

There may, of course, be circumstances where the rights of minorities may conflict with the rights of individuals, even as there are cases where the rights of individuals may conflict with each other; that is not an argument against such rights.

When the UN made the declaration, several countries expressed reservations: they included the US, Canada, Australia and New Zealand (though Australia subsequently accepted the declaration). Those countries are democratic states where governments are fully accountable to law; but they were also founded on the dispossession of indigenous populations. Canada, despite its efforts to redress continuing disadvantage, has been heavily criticised by the United Nations Human Rights Council for its treatment of its aboriginal population:

> The relationship of Canada with the indigenous peoples within its borders is governed by a well-developed legal framework and a number of policy initiatives that in many respects are protective of indigenous peoples' rights. ... The numerous initiatives ... have been insufficient. The well-being gap between aboriginal and non-aboriginal people in Canada has not narrowed over the past several years; treaty and aboriginal claims remain persistently unresolved; indigenous women and girls remain vulnerable to abuse; and overall there appear to be high levels of distrust among indigenous peoples towards the government at both the federal and provincial levels.[39]

This kind of problem is not, however, limited to indigenous peoples. Many, possibly most, countries have issues relating to ethnic, religious or tribal differences, often marked not just by disadvantage but by interpersonal violence.

'Family values'. Because families are informal, many of the norms relating to family life are invisible until they are broken – issues such as neglect and abuse, the responsibility to feed a child, sending a child to school and so on. These codes are often presented ideologically as if they were individualist values; that presentation depends on the assumption that families are not a social group, but an expression of individuality. There is a dividing line running between individuals

---

[39] UN Human Rights Council, 2014, Report of the Special Rapporteur on the rights of indigenous peoples James Anaya: The situation of indigenous peoples in Canada, www.ohchr.org/Documents/Issues/IPeoples/SR/A.HRC.27.52.Add.2.doc, last obtained 28 September 2018, p 1.

and families, on one hand, and communities and social networks on the other. That distinction seems more or less to work if we think the issues are about privacy and non-intervention; but many of the values associated with the family are the opposite – they are about being with, living together, sharing and being committed to other people. Family values are collective if they say, for example, that family life is the best way to live; that children are better when they live in stable, supportive families; that not having a family is selfish; that families teach people how to give and take; that the structure of the family is natural, or ordained by God; or that family members are responsible for each other.

Defence and military action. It may seem odd to present issues relating to security, defence and armed force in terms of values, rather than as a collective aim or a consequence of certain collective arrangements, but it is difficult otherwise to understand the depth of people's emotional attachment to these arrangements. The role of the armed forces is partly to be understood in terms of the protection of society and the nation (however that is constructed), partly in terms of culture. Partly, too, there is a sense of reciprocity, sometimes called the 'military covenant'. The armed forces are seen as a public service, putting themselves at risk for the benefit of others; it follows that others owe them a duty of support. Military engagement carries with it a degree of pride, honour and status, quite distinct from the regard that equivalent occupations might have in civilian life – while conversely, soldiers who use their skills and training in commercial or mercenary security operations might be seen in some way as compromising that sense of public service.

At the outset of this chapter I pointed to the links between collective thought and the values of socialism. Two of the examples I have just given are politically 'conservative' – associated with the traditional right wing of politics – and an emphasis on culture, tradition and heritage might well be conservative, too. It is questionable whether political ideologies of collectivism, such as those emphasising local collectives or those which want to extend moral responsibilities across communities, can sensibly be considered 'left wing'. There is a genuine tension here. Socialist values are often phrased in universalist terms; one of the core arguments for equality, and indeed for many varieties of social justice, is an argument for consistency, demanding that people in similar circumstances should be treated in similar ways. But collective values are often communitarian rather than universalist: they are located in specific societies and specific social relationships.

In practice, mainstream ideologies like conservatism or social democracy all tend to be pragmatic, alternating between individualist and collectivist perspectives according to circumstances. There does not need to be a contradiction. Collectivism is a part of everyday life, and that applies to people across the political spectrum. But communitarian values need to be counterbalanced with some universalist principles, to ensure that individuals and minorities are protected. Values such as loyalty and identity need to be coupled with other principles, such as fairness, tolerance and empowerment; without them, collectivism can become hierarchical, exclusive and repressive. The recognition of individual and minority rights – such as rights to dignity, respect or access to the conditions of civilisation – is an essential safeguard for the position of every person within a community.

9

Policies for the common good

The common good

There are many different conceptions of the good, and people's understanding of the common good is no clearer or more coherent than for any other type of good. Part of the idea of the common good is concerned with what is 'good'; consequentialist morality has tended to associate that with particular interests. Hayek identifies collectivism with the pursuit of a single social end:

> The common features of all collectivist systems may be described ... as the deliberate organisation of the labours of society for a definite social goal. ... The 'social goal', or 'common purpose', for which society is to be organised, is usually vaguely described as the 'common good', or the 'general welfare', or the 'general interest'.[1]

Even if we leave aside the internal contradiction – a 'definite' social goal that is only 'vaguely' described – this is not true of all forms of collectivism, by any means. Some forms of collectivism are about social organisation, not about social objectives. Some are about principles of action. The common good might be said to be about consequences, but within that broad range there are still many different senses. Michael Oakeshott argued that there were three prominent accounts of the term: a 'religious' view that emphasised righteousness or moral virtue; a 'productivist' view, emphasising prosperity or wealth; and a 'distributionist' view, emphasising security or welfare.[2] (Oakeshott was another conservative individualist; he rejected all three.)

The common good might be represented in the first place as the sum of particular interests. (This is often mistakenly identified with the sum of individual interests; of course, there is no intention to exclude

---

[1]   F Hayek, 1944, *The road to serfdom*, London: Routledge, pp 59–60.
[2]   M Oakeshott, 1993, *Morality and politics in modern Europe*, New Haven, CT: Yale University Press, pp 92 ff.

the interests of corporate businesses, but there is sometimes a naive assumption that corporate businesses must ultimately act in the interests of individuals.) This is one of the most prominent understandings of the common good, and the approach which dominates formal economics.

The problem with this idea is that interests may conflict with each other. Individuals differ in their preferences and criteria for their wellbeing. Many interests are not shared or held in common, and there are liable to be problems as soon as particular interests are recognised. That is true partly because there may be inconsistencies in the way that preferences are expressed,[3] but mainly because where there are differences, any actions taken will be for the good of some people, not for everyone. Unless we can all agree about what is good, the common good cannot be the good of everyone. This is the core weakness in utilitarianism, which promotes the happiness of the community by balancing people's interests against each other[4] – prompting the obvious objection that some people might be worse off as a result. Cost–Benefit Analysis (CBA), the main formal application of this approach, only appears to maximise total social value.[5] CBA works by assuming that gainers will compensate losers, even if they don't. Conversely, considering when it is in the common interest to avoid something bad, the same criticisms apply. CBA can calculate whether total value goes down, but it disregards how the loss is distributed.

The main alternative to CBA in economic theory has been the criterion of Pareto efficiency: the idea that a group is better off if at least one person has more, and no one else has less.[6] The test must make sense to some, because so many writers use it, but it is deeply flawed. Improving resources only for some people changes their relative purchasing power, and that also affects the people whose resources have not improved. Probably the simplest example of this is in access to land: rich people can use their property rights to keep poor people away. The same principle applies in other contexts. A study in the

---

[3] K Arrow, 1967, Values and collective decision making, in E Phelps (ed) *Economic justice*, Harmondsworth: Penguin.

[4] J Bentham (1789) *An introduction to the principles of morals and legislation*, Oxford: Blackwell, 1960, p 127; and see N Bowie, R Simon, 1977, *The individual and the political order*, Englewood Cliffs, NJ: Prentice-Hall.

[5] e.g. Independent Evaluation Group, 2010, *Cost benefit analysis in World Bank projects*, Washington, DC: World Bank.

[6] e.g. R Sugden, 1981, *The political economy of public choice*, Oxford: Martin Robertson, p 3; J Griffin, 1986, *Well-being*, Oxford: Oxford University Press, p 147.

Philippines offers an illustration. When poor families with children received benefits in cash, they bought more protein-rich food. Malnutrition in those families reduced, but the price of the food went up. Families who were not getting the benefits had to pay more for the food, so their consumption of protein-rich food got worse, and so did the nutrition of their children.[7] Prices are relative: the effect of offering scarce resources to some and not others is that those who gain will be able to get those things before others do. If inequalities increase, some people will be worse off. The common good cannot mean only that some people gain, and others do not; there has to be some mechanism by which the benefits are shared.

A second view of the common good is based on 'common ground', or interests which coincide with the interests of other people. This also depends on particular interests, but only those interests that are shared – in everyday life, people often do share interests. In some cases, that happens simply because they live together – the closer people are to each other, the more they share. People who live in the same house have some interests in common; people who live in the same street, people who live in the same part of town, all the way up to people who live in the same country (and beyond), have interests which relate to their common location and circumstances. The clearest case in theoretical terms is the example of 'public goods', a relatively narrow class of exceptions which are 'non-rival' (that is, not mutually exclusive) and non-excludable (so that anyone can benefit from them). Examples are roads, parks and street lighting.[8] However, these are only the most obvious example of common ground; common interests are much wider than a focus on public goods suggests. Services such as medical services, banking or food distribution depend on a social and economic infrastructure. The 'institutional' concept of welfare is based on the idea that everyone is potentially subject at different times to common social 'states of dependency'. Everyone is liable at some point to be a child, sick or old; everyone is subject to risks such as interrupted income or disability.[9] The resources that people are able

---

[7] D Filmer, J Friedman, E Kandpal, J Onishi, 2018, *General equilibrium effects of targeted cash transfers*, Washington, DC: World Bank Group.

[8] S Bailey, 2002, *Public sector economics*, Basingstoke: Palgrave; Core Group, 2017, The economy: public goods, www.core-econ.org/the-economy/book/text/12.html#125-public-goods, last obtained 28 September 2018.

[9] H Wilensky, C Lebeaux, 1965, *Industrial society and social welfare*, New York: Free Press, ch 6; R Titmuss, 1963, Essays on 'the welfare state', London: Allen and Unwin, pp 42–4.

to draw on depends on what is available for their neighbours and the communities they live in as well as on their own situation.

It is possible to argue that measures that promote the shared interests of some – policies for families, communities, segments of the population such as children or old people, or the economy – might still be considered to help everyone. There is a potential problem here. For example, support for older people might be seen as support for everyone, but it has at times been represented as a factional interest that disadvantages younger people. There is a similar problem with infrastructure development. There are parts of the infrastructure such as roads or drains that will never be used by many people, because of where they are located. Putting those reservations in more general terms, if segments represent particular interests, they might be seen as subject to the same weaknesses, and the same objections, as the arguments relating to the sum of particular interests. The main way to avoid this implication is to make services more general and more universal. The more widely the net is cast, the less persuasive it becomes to think about shared interests in individual terms. The existence of general standards is a benefit for everyone, and there is a common interest in maintaining them. It is in the interests of each and every person that there should be sanitation, running water and an energy supply. General ill health, standing water through lack of drainage or a poor waste management expose everyone to risks, not only the people who lack facilities. Crime rates – both crimes against people and crimes against property – make everyone's life more difficult. A population who cannot read can create problems for employers and modern industry. And concentrations of poverty affect everyone in a poor area, not just the people who are individually poor.

By this account, any person is likely to have two different sets of interests: particular interests which are held individually, and the common interests shared with other people in society. Madison's definition of a 'faction' depends on a recognition that the interests of some can conflict with the 'permanent and aggregate' interests of the whole community.[10] Rousseau, who identified the common good with the 'general will', argued: 'There is often a considerable difference between the will of all and the general will. The latter is concerned only with the common interest, the former with interests that are partial, being itself but the sum of individual wills.'[11] Unless the interests of

---

[10] J Madison, 1788, *Federalist papers 10*, New York: Mentor, 1961, p 78.

[11] J-J Rousseau, 1762, The social contract, in E Barker (ed) *Social contract*, Oxford: Oxford University Press, 1971, book II, ch 3, p 193.

each person square exactly with the interests of the community, there will be some interests that the person has individually, and those which each person has as a member of society. That implies, in turn, that there is a social interest, a common interest that is distinct and potentially different from the interests of individuals or particular groups.

The observation that people have such interests in common does not imply that their common interests override every other sort of interest. There is always some potential for conflict between perceptions of the common good and the good of particular individuals and groups. Personal violence, poverty, war and pollution are generally bad for everyone. There may be some people who benefit from them individually, and choose for them to happen – that is because for them the benefits outweigh the cost – but they still experience the detriment to some extent. There are others where they do not benefit, and the common good becomes the more important consideration. When sewers were being introduced in the 1850s, there was active opposition from some ratepayers who were concerned that they would have to bear the costs (Palmerston, the Prime Minister, called them 'the dirty party'[12]). In others, individual rights may prevail. There are circumstances where individual preferences outweigh the public cost – traffic congestion is an illustration. And there are cases when the cost to some individuals is too high. Benn and Peters suggest, for example, that 'the common good of defence might not be a good enough reason for uprooting a hundred families to make a rocket range. It might be better to compromise for the benefit of the few.'[13] Conflicts of interest do not invalidate the idea of a common good, but the common good may not be the only good that is being considered.

The third view of the common good is exclusively collective. It identifies the common good with the public interest, the good of society as a whole. It can reasonably be argued that a good society is a better place to live for everyone, but that cannot be taken for granted. Economic development, the education of children or the maintenance of order are helpful to the community that one is part of, but they will not necessarily be helpful to every particular named individual. For example, educating the future workforce may not mean much to a childless, older person (even if that person did benefit from a similar policy when young); there are some people who will not be directly touched by those issues.

---

[12] S Finer, 1952, *The life and times of Edwin Chadwick*, London: Methuen.

[13] S Benn, R Peters, 1959, *Social principles and the democratic state*, London: George Allen and Unwin, p 272.

Some policies are directly intended to further the maintenance and reproduction of society as a whole. Examples are the stewardship of the environment for future generations, and defence. The report of an independent commission on American foreign policy felt able to identify a hierarchy of national interests, all intended to strengthen 'the ability of the US government to safeguard and enhance the well-being of Americans in a free and secure nation':

- 'Vital national interests are conditions that are strictly necessary' for this capacity. Examples included deterring or reducing the possibility of nuclear, biological or chemical weapons attacks on the US or promoting relations with Russia and China.
- 'Extremely important national interests are conditions that, if compromised, would severely prejudice but not strictly imperil' this capacity. They include, for example, the promotion of stability in the Western hemisphere, the prevention of genocide and the suppression of terrorism. (This was written before the first major terrorist attack on the US.)
- 'Important national interests are conditions that, if compromised, would have major negative consequences.' They include 'massive' human rights violations in other countries, and maximising growth from US trade and foreign investment.
- 'Secondary national interests … are important and desirable conditions, but ones that have little direct impact' on this capacity. They include expanding democracy and enhancing US exports.[14]

Regardless of the specific claims and the ranking of interests, which is often controversial, it is striking to see such a strong statement of collective interests made on behalf of a country that is so often associated with the values of atomistic, liberal individualism. The rationale for the appraisal is strictly collectivist – the nature of the interests, understood from the perspective of the country as a whole. The argument is probably clearest in the case of common 'bads', like being invaded or torn apart by civil strife. The presence of a defence force is not an unequivocal good, but its absence or insufficiency can be catastrophic.

There are often conflicting interpretations of collective interests: the discussion of economic development in Box 9.1 is illustrative. However, these different understandings of the common good do not have to be

---

[14]   The Commission on America's National Interests, 2000, *America's national interests*, Cambridge, MA: Belfer Center for Science and International Affairs.

seen as mutually exclusive. The wellbeing of each and every person matters for the welfare of all of us. Every member of a family shares, to some extent, the pleasure and pain of others; it is hardly possible for a family to be content and satisfied with their circumstances when a child is dangerously ill. In the same way, it is difficult for the members of a society to be content if the most vulnerable people in that society are suffering. There are differences, of course, between families and societies; the relationship we have to members of our family is closer and stronger than it is to others. But wherever other people lack welfare, it affects us, too. Poverty and inequality make life worse, not just for the poor, but for everyone. A society where people die early, where they are homeless or excluded, is a worse place to live for everyone else. As *The Spirit Level* shows, societies that are more unequal are less healthy, more prone to crime and poorer than others.[15]

Box 9.1: Economic development

Economic development is usually seen as a good thing. Where there is no development, countries remain mired in poverty. There are some people who think that 'development stinks'[16] – that it is offering poor countries a 'deceitful mirage'.[17] They are wrong. Development increases the resources available to a society, and with those resources comes a wide range of benefits: better health, better education, more personal safety, a better physical environment. Roads, telecommunications and drainage and electricity help to make everyone's lives better.

There are, however, legitimate concerns about economic development. The first is whether economic growth can be said to be an improvement in itself. The measurement of economic development in terms of GDP per capita has several key flaws. The figures disregard good things that are not based in economic transactions, such as family care. GDP includes undesirable social activity: when a child leaves school to scrape a living on the street, it adds to GDP.[18] It includes not only bad things, but 'anti-bads', too. More money spent on policing, prisons and drug abuse centres all add to economic activity.[19]

---

[15] R Wilkinson, K Pickett, 2009, *The spirit level*, London: Allen Lane.

[16] G Esteva, cited in J Pieterse, 2000, After post development, *Third World Quarterly* 21 (2) 175–91, p 176.

[17] M Rahnema, V Bawtree (eds) 1977, *The post development reader*, London: Zed, p. x.

[18] M Todaro, S Smith, 2011, *Economic development*, Harlow: Pearson.

[19] N Hicks, P Streeten, 1979, Indicators of development: the search for a basic needs yardstick, *World Development* 7 567–80.

The second is whether it can actually be said to be improving the lives of the whole population. The claim is made that 'a rising tide lifts all boats', but as Mishra comments, it can smash some and beach others.[20] The effect of averaging sums over a population is to disregard some of the extreme inequalities in societies, particularly those where rich natural resources are held by a limited few. The World Bank issued papers that claimed that 'growth is good for the poor', because on average poor people gained proportionately from growth[21] – that is, people who were on the bottom rung of the ladder may still be on the bottom rung, but at least they were not worse off. That still leaves the problem that some of those poor people will be worse off, even as some are better off. Economic development leads to change in many ways: it is commonly associated with migration from rural to urban societies, with the practices of industrialisation, and with growing inequality. Migration to the cities is often marked by the exclusion of some people from urban land use, squatting and competition for urban space, and poor physical conditions.

Development is not just about money. It is about the way that people live – housing, education, living in communities, communications, employment, information, communications, opportunities and so on. For Amartya Sen, development increases not only the resources that people have, but their capabilities, their choices and their opportunities; it is a matter of freedom.[22]

A fourth view of the common good is based not just on common interests, however those are understood, but on the realisation of those interests through collective action. I referred before to such issues as sanitation, drinking water and energy. Those might be provided collectively, but they might also be distributed through private transactions. While it may be possible in exceptional cases to provide things like sanitation or energy in isolation from others in society, in practical terms it is only in conjunction with others that they can be realised. (This also gives the lie to one of Olson's contentions, that

[20] R Mishra, 1994, The study of poverty in North America, CROP/UNESCO symposium on regional state-of-the-art reviews on poverty research, Paris.

[21] D Dollar, A Kraay, 2000, Growth is good for the poor, http://documents. worldbank.org/curated/en/419351468782165950/Growth-is-good-for-the-poor, last obtained 28 September 2018; D Dollar, T Kleineberg, A Kraay, 2013, Growth still is good for the poor, World Bank, https://openknowledge.worldbank.org/ handle/10986/16001, last obtained 28 September 2018.

[22] A Sen, 2001, *Development as freedom*, Oxford: Oxford University Press.

people will only choose to join small groups.[23] These things cannot be done very easily or effectively by small groups.)

The effect of shifting the emphasis away from consequences and what actions achieve, towards what is done and held in common, has been described as an 'instrumental' concept of the common good.[24] The common good is taken to consist, not of a specific set of policies or outcomes, but in an approach that makes it possible for citizens to achieve their own conception of the good (or at least to avoid things that are bad). In liberal political regimes, that is usually taken to imply a considerable degree of personal freedom and a limited role for government. Rawls argues that people can only agree to a 'thin theory of the good', consisting of certain 'primary goods' – rights, liberties, powers, opportunities, income and wealth.[25] There is a case (put, for example, by J S Mill) for collective action that actively increases people's personal capacity and promotes autonomous action:

> When a government provides means of fulfilling a certain end, leaving individuals free to avail themselves of different means if in their opinion preferable, there is no infringement of liberty, no irksome or degrading restraint.[26]

For Jordan, 'The common good is actively created by citizens participating together in some shared process.'[27] The common good is expressed as a joint sense of purpose, and relies on the exercise of political power to create the conditions for the common good to be pursued. Downing and Thigpen argue that the concept of the common good needs to be seen in terms of a political or deliberative process, rather than a specific prescription for society. People do not need to share a conception of the common good to work towards it; the idea can legitimately be the source of competing policies and interpretations. At the same time, they question whether a liberal state can legitimately require citizens to engage, for example, in a work ethic, or in religious activity; either of those would go further than the choice and autonomy of the citizens would allow.[28]

---

[23] M Olson, 1971, *The logic of collective action*, Cambridge MA: Harvard University Press.

[24] M Murphy, 2005, The common good, *Review of Metaphysics* 59 (1) 133–64.

[25] J Rawls, 1971, *A theory of justice*, Oxford: Oxford University Press, pp 395–9, 62.

[26] J S Mill, 1848, *The principles of political economy*, book 5, ch 11.

[27] B Jordan, 1989, *The common good*, Oxford: Blackwell, p 85.

[28] L Downing, R Thigpen, 1993, Virtue and the common good, *Journal of Politics* 55 (4) 1046–59.

Inevitably, policy which is intended to promote the common good will be linked to specific political actions. Frankel, writing about the 'national interest' in foreign policy, is more cynical. He suggests that the idea might be classified as 'aspirational', 'operational' – that is, identifiable and expedient – or 'explanatory and polemical'. In his view, it is as much a rationalisation for political action as a motivation for it.[29] Benn and Peters question whether there can ever be one vision or one outcome that might be thought of as representing a common good. When two politicians say they are doing something for the common good, they mean to argue that it is not being done to promote a narrow, sectional interest.

> The prescription 'seek the common good' is not of the same type as 'maintain full employment'. Whereas the latter is a counsel of substance, the former is one of procedure. … 'Seek the common good' is different, not because it is vaguer or more general, but because it does not describe a determinate goal at all. It is an instruction to approach policy-making in a certain spirit, not to adopt a determinate policy.[30]

The conditions for a common good

The discussion of substantive collectivism in Chapter 1 is based on the world as it is now. The kinds of arrangement that it refers to – a world of independent, corporate bodies and legal persons – developed over long periods of time. The 'civil rights' claimed in the seventeenth century and eighteenth century included provisions that in their time were radical and extraordinary: among them, freedom of worship, freedom of assembly (without which collective worship is difficult) and the right to form associations (often done surreptitiously). In France, which has depended heavily on the progressive extension of mutual responsibility, mutual aid societies were illegal when they started; they were forbidden or restricted until 1848; now they are one of the cornerstones of the French system. Turkey, nominally a secular state, has long recognised the status of Islamic waqfs, but only recognised the legal status of its first Christian Church in 2000.

---

[29] J Frankel, 1970, *National interest*, London: Pall Mall.
[30] S Benn, R Peters, 1959, *Social principles and the democratic state*, London: Allen and Unwin, p 273.

Marshall saw the development of civil and political rights as a precursor of the social rights that subsequently emerged in the formation of the welfare states.[31] Historically, that is questionable. The English experience was influential, but it was not a pattern that everyone followed. The experience of European countries was often very different: social rights and mutual associations were established before political enfranchisement. The development of welfare services in Germany under Bismarck offered social rights in a relatively newly established country which had neither civil nor political rights.

Paradoxically, in view of their importance for collective action and the common good, these rights – social, civil and political – were conceived as the rights of individuals. There were other attempts in other places to assert collective rights without also protecting individuals: that was done in communist countries and in fascist ones. The failure of collective organisations to flourish under those conditions suggests that the relationship between individual and collective rights is closer than may be apparent at first. If rights cannot be exercised by individuals, the collective cannot stand; individuals can be broken away from the collective, piece by piece, until there is nothing left. So a discussion of the common good has to think, too, about the situation and status of individuals.

The first of these conditions is that people have to be citizens. Citizens are members of a political community, sharing a common status and rights. Marshall defines citizenship as 'a status bestowed on those who are full members of a community. All those who possess the status are equal with respect to the rights and duties with which the status is endowed.'[32] Following Marshall, the idea of citizenship has been broadened out to include social and economic rights as well as political and legal ones. There is, however, an intrinsic problem with the notion: defining people as citizens implicitly defines others as non-citizens. Citizenship is necessarily exclusive as well as inclusive. If the right to welfare is based on membership of a community, there must be those who are not considered members, and so who are not citizens. Often, they are people of different races, different nationalities or (as in much of Europe) migrant workers.

The second condition is a degree of equality. In this book I have not used the language of 'horizontal' and 'vertical' collectivism, which attempts to distinguish collectives where members have equal

---

[31] T Marshall, 1963, Citizenship and social class, in *Sociology at the crossroads*, London: Heinemann.
[32] Marshall, 1963, p 87.

status from other collectives which are hierarchically organised.[33] The problem with those terms is that social groups are mainly about something else: people occupy roles in a group, such as roles in the family, education, work or associations, and most specific roles – father, teacher, employee, board member – are highly differentiated. The language of equality does not have much to do with group membership as such. Equality is primarily concerned with the removal of disadvantage. For a common good to be meaningful, people should not be subject to such disadvantages that they are effectively excluded from participation in the community. The most basic idea of equality is about the 'equality of persons', sometimes called the equality of conditions: that people should not be treated differently on the basis of personal characteristics such as birth or race. With one main exception, this principle has come to command widespread assent, to the point where it is scarcely challenged in contemporary politics: hardly anyone would want to assert a basic difference between aristocrats and peasants, or between different racial categories of the sort that existed in apartheid South Africa. That is extraordinary, because those distinctions have been accepted for much of human history.

The main exception to the trend is gender; there are still many societies where people are only too ready to justify inequalities between men and women. White and his colleagues identify the issue of gender as one of the main factors compromising or obstructing efforts to develop community-led solutions in developing countries:

> Women are only half as likely as men to be aware of [community-driven development] programmes, even less likely to attend the community meetings and even more less likely to speak at them. Gendered cultural norms and socio-economic factors powerfully and negatively influenced the participation of women in the public sphere. … Women's participation challenged traditional power relations that men have in the public domain. … Male relatives may control voting decisions, precluding women's participation in [community development committees], or de-prioritise projects favoured by or benefiting women. … For empowering communities, it would be imperative to have objectives that translate into measures for encouraging

---

[33] T Singelis, H Triandis, D Bawuk, M Gelfand, 1995, Horizontal and vertical dimensions of individualism and collectivism, *Cross-Cultural Research* 29 (3) 240–75.

the participation of women and other marginalised populations.[34]

The idea of 'community-driven' development rings somewhat hollow when half the potential members of a community are marginalised or excluded at the outset.

The importance of equality in this context goes beyond the equality of persons. Participation in society depends on equality in a more substantial sense: poverty has been described as a condition of exclusion from the patterns of life that are open to others. If people are not able to make contact with others, to assemble and to associate, their capacity for collective action is accordingly reduced, and there is a great deal of evidence that links poverty with that sort of reduced capacity. The World Bank's studies *Voices of the poor* identify a series of problems with the social relationships of the poor: common problems include relative physical isolation, lack of power, weak community organisations, gender discrimination and social exclusion.[35]

That leads to a third condition, which is inclusion. The concepts of inclusion and exclusion developed in France, where the main emphasis fell on solidarity and mutual responsibility; people were included in society if they were part of solidaristic social networks, and excluded if they were left out, or shut out, from such arrangements. In more recent work, the United Nations has adopted the idea with a subtle but important modification: social inclusion should imply that no one is left behind. That emphasises that inclusion is not just about the networks that exist in society, but about the rights of the excluded person. The corollary of an emphasis on the common good is that everyone should benefit, and not everyone will benefit if some people can be left out.

A fourth condition is based on a community's ability to develop a shared concept of the common good. Part of the justification for this kind of engagement is instrumental: common action is taken to have beneficial effects. Part of that depends on the idea of equality, considered before; part, too, depends on the exercise of power, 'so as to create conditions for active participation and self rule. But power used to further the interests of individuals and groups corrupts society

---

[34] H White, R Menon, H Waddington, 2018, Community-driven development: does it build social cohesion or infrastructure?, International Initiative for Impact Evaluation, pp 23–5, www.3ieimpact.org/media/filer_public/2018/03/12/wp30-cdd.pdf, last obtained 28 September 2018.

[35] D Narayan, R Chambers, M Shah, P Petesch, 2000, *Voices of the poor: Crying out for change*, New York: World Bank/Oxford University Press.

and destroys the common good.'[36] One of the key issues that direct democracy has been supposed to address is the disadvantage of certain groups: people and communities who have been excluded from political and economic processes. Beyond that, however, participation and engagement have claims to be seen as a good in themselves.

Methods: voice and empowerment

The idea of voice, imported from the language of business, has become one of the key concepts in studies of poverty. If democracy depends on deliberation and free expression, then enabling people to express a voice, and to identify the things that matter to them, is crucial to redressing the imbalance of power that is implicit in elite politics. The work of Robert Chambers in rural development was hugely influential.[37] Chambers found ways of engaging people, asking them what they knew and pooling their knowledge. His advice was to sit, listen, watch, learn, forget the preconceptions, ask, be nice to people and to 'hand over the stick' – give control to people to define their own issues. People know more than they are given credit for. One comment from a participant helps to make the point: 'And we thought we were so foolish because we could not write. Yet look, we had all this information inside us.'[38] *Voices of the poor* was based on a massive exercise of qualitative, participative research – more than 20,000 people responded to queries in 23 countries.[39] The studies played an important part in shifting views of poverty in international organisations from a narrow focus on income towards a multidimensional view of poverty, with a strong emphasis on social relationships.

Participation in decision making, like any form of political engagement, has to have some mechanism or process by which it can take place. It is not enough to know that people have a range of views – the murmurings of the 'street'; there needs to be some way in which those views can be expressed effectively. One of the ways in which this is conventionally done is to find a place for a 'representative' voice – tenants in housing associations, patients in health care, workers on boards and so on. This may widen the range of views under consideration, but it does not make that certain. Another approach is to consult stakeholders and the people

---

[36] Jordan, 1989, p 85.
[37] R Chambers, 1983, *Rural development*, London: Longman.
[38] R Chambers, 1997, *Whose reality counts?* London: Intermediate Technology Publications, p 130.
[39] Narayan et al, 2000.

affected more broadly. Consultation is often treated dismissively in the literature,[40] but is increasingly important for incorporating different perspectives in the process of deliberation. Some consultations are done in the form of representative surveys, which offer a count of responses to set questions: the approaches are vulnerable to common problems of survey design, but, more importantly, the questions may not reflect the issues that people would otherwise wish to raise. Consultations based on open-ended qualitative questions have proved rather more effective. The basic test of a consultation is not that it represents the population numerically, but that it captures a diversity of views. That process is often enhanced by activists offering different perspectives, and the work of umbrella groups that collate views from a range of people and organisations.

Voice is not sufficient to promote empowerment, but it is a major part of it. Empowerment as a concept is both individual and collective: it refers to 'the mechanism by which people, organisations and communities gain mastery over their lives'.[41] This is often seen in the literature as an activity which needs to be mediated by a professional: empowerment is 'a process whereby the social worker or other helping professional engages in a set of activities with the client aimed at reducing the powerlessness stemming from the experience of discrimination because the client belongs to a stigmatised collective'.[42] This kind of approach is seen in the idea of community work, considered before in Box 5.1. Community work is usually aimed – as the name suggests – at communities, though in practice it is often set up in places that don't have much of a community in the hope that there might eventually be one. The central problem with this kind of collective action is not in the concept; it is that it begins from a position of disadvantage, often associated with low resources, and the struggle is always uphill.

Policies for the common good

A huge range of policies might potentially further the common good. In the first place, from the preceding argument, there need to be policies to meet the preconditions: citizenship, equality and inclusion.

---

[40]   e.g. S Arnstein, 1971, A ladder of citizen participation, *Journal of the Royal Town Planning Institute* 57 (4) 176–82.

[41]   Rappaport 1984, cited in L Holdsworth, 1991, *Empowerment social work with physically disabled people*, Norwich: University of East Anglia Social Work Monographs, p 3.

[42]   B Solomon, 1976, *Black empowerment*, New York: Columbia University Press, p 29.

There need to be rights to make sure that people are not left out, measures to protect people from poverty and discrimination, and security for the status of citizens. Some social policies are there for social groups. Family policy is made to protect, promote and regulate family structures: examples are rules about parental responsibility, adoption, substitute family care, family benefits and child protection. Urban policy is concerned with the management of spatial relationships such as access, land use, communications and transport, economic development and community development. Policies concerned with minority ethnic groups, such as the indigenous peoples of the US, Canada or Australia, consider the collective rights and culture of minorities, coupled with measures to redress the disadvantages they suffer.

Some social policies are more universal, in the sense that they potentially benefit everyone. Preventative health care, considered in Box 9.2, is an example. Some other examples have been referred to in discussing conceptions of the common good: sanitation, roads, water and energy supplies. Policies for environmental protection are mainly focused on the health and living conditions of everyone. Universal health coverage provides everyone with the equivalent of personal medical insurance – which might be seen as a public good, but it could equally be deemed to have a value attributable to each and every individual. Policing, at least in countries where it is done properly, offers direct benefits for personal security (regrettably, there are rather too many countries where it has the opposite effect). Arguably, although they are not universal in quite the same way, minimum standards – such as those for food safety, building regulation, unfit housing or social assistance – have a similarly beneficial effect for everyone. Supporting a recent paper on Universal Basic Services, Henrietta Moore argued that providing people universally with free services, such as free transport or wi-fi communication, 'will make accessible a life that includes participation, builds belonging and common purpose, and potentially strengthens the cohesion of society as a whole'.[43] The language she has chosen to make the point is infused with collectivist values.

Then there are policies for the whole of society – policies concerned with governance, the maintenance of order and the reproduction of society. Defence and the armed forces have a continuing role to ensure territorial security. Systems of education are a benefit for the individuals engaged with them, but beyond that they have an

---

[43] H Moore, in Institute for Global Prosperity, 2017, Universal basic services, https://www.ucl.ac.uk/bartlett/igp/files/universal-basic-services-radical-proposal-ucls-institute-global-prosperity, last obtained 28 September 2018.

important role in shaping the character and structure of the future society. Much the same is true of policies aimed at culture and the arts; individuals may benefit, but a major part of the agenda is the development and maintenance of a culture into the future. The stewardship of the environment is a responsibility not just to conserve, but to build for future generations.

Box 9.2: Preventative health care

Preventative health care is conventionally divided between primary prevention, which stops a person from developing a problem in the first place, and secondary prevention, which involves identifying problems in their early stages before they become serious.

Much of what is done by way of primary prevention is not necessarily classifiable as health care: it may imply regulation (for example, regulation on air quality), taxation (used to deter people from smoking), even engineering (the basis of sanitation and a clean water supply). Primary prevention may be done by changing the environment, which has been the approach of public health services; changing people's behaviour, attempted through health education, legal restrictions, such as licensing the sale of alcohol, and financial disincentives, such as taxation on cigarettes and alcohol; and changing people's condition. Vaccination is the obvious example; fluoridation of water supplies to avoid dental decay in children is another. The major fatal diseases in Britain – cancer, stroke and heart disease – are all clearly and directly related to smoking. Smoking is also an evident cause of major impairment, including respiratory ailments and circulatory diseases. The UK government's response has been to combine health education with financial disincentives in the form of high taxation, and increasing restrictions on smoking in public places. This has been surprisingly effective; only one adult in six now smokes, a decline of two thirds over 40 years.[44]

Secondary prevention takes place after the problem has occurred. This may happen, for example, through screening of women for breast and cervical cancer,

---

[44] Office for National Statistics, 2017, Adult smoking behaviour in the UK 2016, https://www.ons.gov.uk/peoplepopulationandcommunity/healthandsocialcare/ healthandlifeexpectancies/bulletins/adultsmokinghabitsingreatbritain/2016, last obtained 28 September 2018; D Campbell, 2016, Number of smokers in England drops to all-time low, *Guardian*, 20 September, https://www.theguardian.com/ society/2016/sep/20/number-of-uk-smokers-falls-to-lowest-level, last obtained 28 September 2018.

or advising mothers to have an abortion after amniocentesis identifying that a child may be disabled. Perinatal and infant mortality has been a major concern. The arguments for dealing with maternity in hospital settings have been (on the face of it) to do with prevention; the NHS is supposed to respond better in extreme cases if the mother is in hospital. This is debatable: Finland, with one of the lowest perinatal mortality rates in Europe, also has a much higher rate of home births.

There are aspects of preventative health which might be seen as individualistic. Common patterns of disease – heart disease, diabetes, obesity and dementia – are individual in their nature, and the aggregated statistics do not imply any shared interest and approach, let alone anything like a network or social group. But many of the patterns of response are collective – whether this is done in terms of methodological collectivism, such as screening or shifting the curve, in groups through policies such as fluoridation or school health, or to whole populations in managing air quality or vaccinations.

There are sometimes public debates about whether or not these measures are actually beneficial – protests against fluoridation are common, and there has often been controversy about whether vaccinations damage some children in order to save others. Legislators have been slow to restrain the right of manufacturers to poison people in the name of commerce, but the same inaction has not been evident in the courts; many of the same arguments which have curtailed smoking can be expect to be raised against alcohol or adulteration of products with sugar.

Despite the disagreements, there is little debate about the central principle; as to whether improving the health of the population is a valid aim, the main question is how to do it. Individualists tend to favour individualistic methods: education, health promotion, perhaps a degree of persuasion or 'nudging' people towards desirable conduct.[45] Collectivists tend to argue for measures that shift the curve (an approach discussed in Chapter 2, on methodological collectivism) or a regulatory framework – that is, a common solution for the common good. Establishing general rules may ultimately be less personally intrusive than the 'educational' approach.

There are many good arguments for collective action to achieve these goals. In *Arguments for welfare* I considered twenty-six.[46] They fall into four main classes. First, there are moral arguments. Collective action is morally right if it is consistent with general moral rules, such as human

---

[45]   R Thaler, C Sunstein, 2008, *Nudge*, New Haven, CT: Yale University Press.
[46]   P Spicker, 2017, *Arguments for welfare*, London: Rowman and Littlefield.

rights or the principles of major religions; if it is done in recognition of specific obligations; if it is motivated by benevolence, altruism or humanitarianism; if it expresses a sense of social responsibility, duty or reciprocity. People's needs, rights and humanity ought to be considered. Second, there are economic arguments. Collective provision serves the interests of the population, particularly in circumstances where markets are unable to provide effectively – and there are many such cases. It makes it possible to invest in people, manage the economy and promote human development. Third, there are pragmatic reasons. Governments have the capacity, the resources and the people to do important jobs; and public services have proved to be the most practical way of providing for populations comprehensively, universally or to meet needs that are not met otherwise. Fourth, there are collective and mutualist arguments. Self-interested people cooperate. Pooling resources and pooling risks are tried and tested ways of increasing capacity and reducing vulnerability.

Despite marked differences in political beliefs, approaches and circumstances, there is hardly a government in the world that does not accept at least some of these arguments. Social protection, economic management, infrastructure development, emergency planning and basic security are not done uniformly or always well, but the idea that governments ought to be doing these things is now so widespread that they can legitimately be described as a standard part of the functions of contemporary government. Why should collective action become the province of government, rather than remaining the preserve of the voluntary, mutualist and other independent providers who otherwise do these things? Part of the reason for this is practical: government is there and has the capacity to act. Part is about accountability: government is accountable for its actions, and sensitive to issues, such as press coverage and the preferences of voters, which is unlikely to be true of private corporations or many social institutions. But the basic arguments in principle are about universality and inclusion. Solidaristic, mutualist arrangements leave gaps. If people think there ought to be minimum standards, or universal provision, or at least systems that do not exclude people, only governments have the capacity and authority to bring this about. There are powerful moral imperatives at work; this is what democratic governments are there for.

10

The common weal

Towards a good society

Individualism and collectivism are not incompatible, mutually exclusive views; they are simply different ways of looking at social issues. They coexist, because people in society are at one and the same time both individuals and members of groups. In epistemological terms, people might act individually at some points, and at others they act in a group role. There are times when only an individual or collective perspective will explain what is happening, but there are others where there is a choice to be made. In moral terms, too, individualist and collectivist accounts both have to be taken into account. Individual responsibility does not excuse collective groups from moral judgment, any more than collective action exempts the individuals who participate in it. The idea of 'dualism' has mainly been used to describe the epistemology,[1] but I think it can be extended to cover the moral issues, too. Moral individualism is important as a protection for the position of individuals in relation to groups; at the same time, moral collectivism is important for understanding group responsibility.

The arguments that I have made in this book are compatible with a wide range of approaches to policy. That is only to be expected; much of the political mainstream, including conservatism, socialism and social democracy, is built on principles that recognise the force of individualist, collectivist and social perspectives at the same time. In my previous work on individualism, I pointed to three very broad areas of activity legitimately implied by an emphasis on individuals: rights, basic security and empowerment. In the discussion of collectivism, I have pointed to the importance of political participation, solidarity and social inclusion. These are different agendas, but they have a substantial overlap, and even in areas where they are distinct – the individualist emphasis on basic security, or the collectivist emphasis

---

[1]   R Sawyer, 2005, *Social emergence*, Cambridge: Cambridge University Press, ch 5.

on inclusion – they can be seen as mutually reinforcing rather than as contradictory.

It is possible to construct the issues negatively – to use both individualism and collectivism as implying a critique of the other dimension – but it may be more helpful to look at the ways they can strengthen each other. In the first place, there are areas which seem to be substantially different. Issues like basic security, dignity and respect for persons belong primarily in the field of individualism – a belief that each and every person is valuable in their own right. Issues such as social inclusion, social cohesion and stewardship belong primarily in the field of collectivism – a belief that social relationships also need to be nurtured and protected.

Then there are areas which are held by both individualists and collectivists, but are liable to be understood differently in the light of the different focuses. Individual freedom emphasises choice and autonomous action; collective freedom emphasises capacity and collective empowerment. The individualist views of equality are likely to compare individuals to other individuals, and emphasise the equality of opportunity and the removal of barriers; collectivist views of equality are likely to compare blocs, and emphasise the equality of welfare or of outcomes.

There are also, beyond those categories, some areas of common concern and overlap, where it is difficult to make any firm distinctions between individual and collective positions. There are individualists and collectivists who accept the rule of law, the place of religion, the case for democratic deliberation, communitarian morality and human rights.[2] That is not, I think, simply because we can accommodate those ideas within a spectrum of views from the individual to the collective; it is because many collectivists accept the protections of individualism (such as human rights and equality before the law), while individualists recognise the collective character of social interaction (including religion and morality). I have argued that individualism has to be tempered by the reality of social interaction and relationships. Considering the position of collectivism here, it should be clear that the converse is also true. Collectivism cannot be permitted to override the value of the individual, any more than individualism should be allowed to override responsibilities to social groups and society.

---

[2]   e.g. A Etzioni, 2004, *The common good*, Malden, MA: Polity Press.

At the end of Chapter 3, I suggested that the central moral question for collectivists is, 'what makes a good society?' I think there is enough here to offer the beginnings of an answer to that question.

The first step depends on a recognition of how people live. Neither individualism nor collectivism are intrinsically good or bad – they are perspectives, not moral rules. Either could be deeply damaging if taken to extremes. Exclusive individualism, of the sort favoured by Thoreau,[3] implies an atomised society with diminished social contact and a loss of the benefits of cooperation. Exclusive collectivism, discussed in Box 3.2, is a horror.

Next, there are certain principles that are needed to be able to realise an effective balance between individual and collective approaches. There are the preconditions of the common good, including citizenship, a degree of equality, social inclusion and rights; and there is the pursuit of the common good in itself, through mutuality, community and awareness of our interdependence.

Third, there are methods intended to deal with the imbalances of power and regulate the conduct of society. They cover the institutions of democracy – including the rule of law, accountability and rights – and processes of engagement, deliberation, voice and empowerment.

Peter Townsend once argued that social policy 'is best conceived as a kind of blueprint for the management of society towards social ends'.[4] Tony Crosland thought this was a 'vulgar fallacy'; too much is unknown and unknowable.[5] 'What makes a good society' is not based on a vision of utopia, but on a range of principles and approaches. None of the principles or methods absolutely guarantees a good outcome. The best that can be said is that trying to do things better bit by bit, difficult though it may be, should lead, however falteringly, to a better state. The same is true when answering the question, 'what makes a good person?' Moral conduct is a process, not an absolute state of being.

The principles of the common weal

'Weal' is an ancient word for welfare, and a 'commonweal' – an idea that is nearly as old – is a political community that aims to do things together for the collective welfare. The idea of the 'common weal' might refer to the common good, and it might refer to the wellbeing of everyone; but it also refers to the body politic, and the way that

---

[3] H Thoreau, 1854, Walden, in *The portable Thoreau*, New York: Viking, 1947.
[4] P Townsend, 1976, *Sociology and social policy*, Harmondsworth: Penguin, p 6.
[5] C A Crosland 1956, *The future of socialism*, London: Jonathan Cape, p 216.

things are done. I wrote most of the material that follows for a Scottish political movement, Common Weal. It sums up what I wanted to say in this book, and it seemed appropriate to repeat it here.

Society

We live together in society. People do not live in isolation from each other; we live in families and communities. Most of us belong to a wide range of groups and networks – joined together by, for example, culture, education, religion, mutual responsibility and our shared experiences. A society is a group of all those groups. Many of the things that make life work happen at the level of society as a whole: education, health care, pensions, roads, parks and many other services are organised socially, and they make us all better off than we would be without them.

The common good

We have to act collectively to advance the welfare of everyone. There are many understandings of the common good: they include the improvement of everyone's circumstances individually, the enhancement of the interests that people hold in common, and the interests of a whole society. But the common good is also concerned with the question of how people can work together to achieve common objectives, and a society that tries to advance the common good needs to do it through a process of deliberation and collective action

Solidarity

We have obligations to each other. The idea of 'solidarity' is widely used in Europe to mean that people are held together by bonds of mutual obligation – the ties of family, community and society. People are included in society when they are part of those networks, excluded when they are not. The common weal is an idea that includes people, and binds them together. It means that we are all of us responsible for each other. This does not mean that people are not also responsible for themselves; but it does mean that looking out for oneself is not enough, and never can be. 'All the members of human society', Adam Smith wrote, 'stand in need of each other's assistance.'[6] Every one of us depends on the help and support of others.

---

[6]   A Smith, 1759, *The theory of moral sentiments*, II.ii.3.

Stewardship

We have a duty to future generations. Part of the responsibility we have is to each other. Part is to those who have come before us – to preserve our common heritage. Part is to those who will come after us. Each generation has a duty of stewardship for the generations to come – a duty that goes beyond the narrower idea of 'sustainability', because it is a commitment to make things better, not just to keep things going. The common weal calls for us to build for the future.

Rights

A society has to protect the rights of every person in it. If the wellbeing of each and every person matters for the welfare of all of us, the common weal cannot be achieved by sacrificing the welfare of some people for the good of others. People need a certain amount of personal security and protection against abuse by others, regardless of whether that is done by groups, or just by other people. Rights are important as universal principles, but they also have an important role in regulating social relationships, giving people who hold them the ability to protect their situation and redress the consequences of imbalances of power.

Equality

Everyone needs access to the conditions of civilisation. There are many differences between people – for example, differences of gender, of religion, of physical capacity. Equality means that wherever there are such differences, people should not have to suffer from disadvantages because of them. The most basic type of equality is about respect for persons: people of any kind should not be treated as inferior. Then there is equality of opportunity; people should not be denied opportunities because of who they are. Our common weal calls for equality, however, in a deeper way. The real argument for equality, Tawney argued, was that every person in a society should have 'access to the conditions of civilisation'[7] – including, among other issues, education, housing, sanitation, health care and a basic income.

---

[7] R Tawney, 1930, *Equality*, London: Allen and Unwin, p 122.

A common enterprise

Social development depends on collective action. The common weal depends on common action: 'to build more we must share more.'[8] The common good relies on the exercise of political power to create the conditions for it be achieved. We are part of a joint enterprise, which every person contributes to, so that every person can benefit. By working together, every one of us can achieve more than we can do alone. And acting together has another, less immediate advantage: when people cooperate, they have the opportunity to build a community, and identity, and a sense of solidarity.

---

[8] Common Weal, 2017, Vision, http://allofusfirst.org/vision, last obtained 28 September 2018.

Index

Index of names